Frederick William Thomas

The Mutual Influence of Muhammadans and Hindus in Law, Morals, and Religion

during the period of Muhammadan ascendancy. Being the 'Le Bas' prize

essay for 1891

Frederick William Thomas

The Mutual Influence of Muhammadans and Hindus in Law, Morals, and Religion
during the period of Muhammadan ascendancy. Being the 'Le Bas' prize essay for
1891

ISBN/EAN: 9783337130220

Printed in Europe, USA, Canada, Australia, Japan

Cover: Foto ©ninafisch / pixelio.de

More available books at **www.hansebooks.com**

THE MUTUAL INFLUENCE

OF

MUHAMMADANS AND HINDUS

IN LAW, MORALS, AND RELIGION DURING THE
PERIOD OF MUHAMMADAN ASCENDANCY.

BEING THE 'LE BAS' PRIZE ESSAY FOR 1891.

BY

F. W. THOMAS,

TRINITY COLLEGE, CAMBRIDGE.

'Agra and Lahor of great Mogul.'

CAMBRIDGE:

DEIGHTON, BELL AND CO.

LONDON: GEORGE BELL AND SONS.

1892

PREFACE.

THIS essay, which is published in accordance with the conditions attached to the Le Bas Prize, aims at portraying the changes in Law, Morality and Religion, which Muhammadanism caused and sustained during the period of its supremacy in India. Covering so wide a range of research, it is naturally under considerable obligations to previous writers. To enumerate these in full would be superfluous, since specific acknowledgments are made at the foot of each page. But that indebtedness which is too considerable to be acknowledged in notes should not be passed over here.

The introductory chapter, which attempts by depicting the characteristics of Hinduism and Muhammadanism to elucidate the conditions of the problem, is of such a nature as to dispense for the most part with references. The pages treating of Hinduism were written almost without consultation of books by the light of previous reading. For the latter portion I have availed myself of many of the best known descriptions of Muhammadanism, in particular of the article in the *Encyclopaedia Britannica*, Hughes' *Dictionary of Islam*, the Quran and the notes of Palmer and Wherry, along with Sale's *Preliminary Discourse*, the Lives of Mahomet, especially those by Sir William Muir and Syad

Amir Ali, Sir Syad Ahmad Khan's *Essays*, and Sir William Muir's *Annals of the Early Khalifate*. I am under especial obligations to A. von Kremer's *Culturgeschichte des Islam unter den ersten Khalifen;* the same author's *Geschichte der herrschenden Ideen des Islam* I regret not to have had access to.

The chapter on Law and Government is based on the various Histories of India, the native codes Manu Nārada &c., Tod's *Annals of Rajasthan*, the Travels of Hiuen-Thsang, Fa-Hian, and Albirûni, and some general reading of Sanskrit literature and antiquities. On the subject of land-tenure I have made much use of Baden-Powell's *Land-systems of British India*, and Phillips' Tagore Law Lectures for 1875, as well as original documents such as the Ain-i-Akbari and the Fifth Report of 1812.

In the discussions on Morality and Religion the references are from the nature of the case more scattered, and as I have acknowledged in the notes all the indebtedness of which I am conscious, little need be said here. Yet I should make mention of the works of Barth and Monier-Williams and Garcin de Tassy's brief treatise on certain *Particularités de la Religion Musulmane dans l'Inde.* The best accounts of the customs and rites of the Indian Musalmans are contained in Mrs Meer Hassan Ali's *Observations on the Indian Mussulmauns*, 1832, and Herklots' *Qanoon-i-Islam,* published in the same year.

The concluding 'Retrospect and Forecast,' consisting mainly of inference and a summary of present circumstances and prospects, is of a less positive character. The opinions there expressed are, except where otherwise stated, either everyone's or my own, and the whole is open to dispute in a greater measure than the matter of the other chapters. On the subject of the Wahabis I have consulted, beside more obvious sources of information, Burckhardt's *Notes on the Bedouins and Wahabees,*' Brydges' *History of the Wahabis,* and Palgrave's *Travels in Central and Eastern Arabia.* So far as the history of the movement in India is concerned, we have an article in the *Calcutta Review* for 1870, Sir W. W. Hunter's *Our Indian Musalmans,* with the criticisms of Sir Syad Ahmad Khan and Sir Alfred Lyall, and letters by Colonel Nassau Lees and others in the *Times* for 1871. There are also many scattered but authoritative statements in the *Imperial Gazetteer of India* and the *Gazetteer of Bengal.* The writings of Sir Syad Ahmad Khan and Syad Amir Ali represent the advanced school of Indian Musalmans. Mr W. S. Blunt's articles in the *Fortnightly Review* for 1881 and 1884—since republished—contain valuable discussions as to the Present and Future of Islam in India and elsewhere. A like range is covered by Vambéry's well-known work on *Der Islam im 19ten Jahrhundert,* and a short tract by Goergens on *Der Islam und die moderne Kultur.* The political, social, and religious questions are, of course, discussed in the general literature of the day.

Lastly, I am indebted for several suggestions and corrections to those who examined the essay.

So much in acknowledgment of obligations. As regards minor matters, I have endeavoured to be consistent in spelling so far as is possible for one who does not read Persian or Arabic; except that in well-known names the traditional and in quotations the author's spelling have been retained. An apology is due for many defects and errors incidental to the nature and occasion of such an essay.

April, 1892.

CONTENTS.

INTRODUCTORY.

INTRODUCTORY.

THE CHARACTERISTICS OF HINDUISM AND MUHAMMADANISM
AND THE *À PRIORI* POSSIBILITY OF THEIR MUTUAL
INFLUENCE.

SOCIETY in India, replete as it is with strange contrasts, *Hinduism:* is distinguished in the main by the one great contrast be- *Theory and Fact.* tween its theories and its actuality. In the student of its literature nothing excites such permanent interest and surprise as the simplicity and comprehensiveness of the theories of life which it exhibits. Nothing on the other hand conduces so much to uncertainty and error on the part of those who live and rule in India as the complexity and lack of uniformity in the life they see around them. This contradiction, the complete explanation of which will some day mark the triumph of Indian research, has by strangling the growth of native history been the chief barrier to its progress. For how could the native care to paint for posterity a reality which confuted all the theories which he regarded as sacred and inspired? and how can the modern historian seriously recount the legends, moral tales, poetry, history made philosophy, which occupied the pious Hindu narrator?

In general, however, the proximate cause of this phenomenon is not far to seek. At a very remote period influences which it is not possible at present to trace had devolved the control of the native religion into the hands of a priestly caste. In the same hands it has remained to this day. The sciences, which in ancient Greece arose partly under foreign influence at a

period when religion was decaying, in India owed their birth
to the requirements of the service of the gods, and were
nursed in the cradle of Brahmanism. The remarkable solidarity which thus existed between all branches of knowledge
could not but have important results. On the one hand it
tended more and more to accentuate the differences between
the priestly caste and the rest of the people. On the other
hand it communicated that religious tinge which penetrates
all native literature, and, what is most important of all, it cut
off from religion all that was natural and spontaneous, and
encrusted it with theological and philosophical subtleties of
every kind.

If, in spite of all, it is still possible to employ Sanskrit
literature and theology in treating of the history and religion
of India, this is to be explained by two considerations. In
the first place, a literature must after all reflect the larger
mental characteristics of the people in whose midst it is produced. The same intellectual tendencies which shaped the
sacred literature moulded the sacred framework of Hindu
society, and the love of fine distinctions which appears in
Sanskrit grammar, logic, rhetoric, law, and philosophy, is
reflected in the complexity of the rules of caste. Secondly,
the literature has to a greater extent than elsewhere reacted
on society. The intellectual life has always been closely knit
to the practical, and the doctor and priest have generally
acted as minister and judge. The varying aspect of Hindu
society is only a stage in a continuous advance towards uniformity, and, if the direction of this advance has passed into
other hands, this is the fault of chance and not of the system.
Brahmanism is one of the greatest assimilants that the world
has known. Even at the present day, when a hostile influence exercised during eight centuries has given place to an
even more potent solvent, it is said to make more converts
than all the other religions in India together. A wild tribe
adopts an ancestor, a priest, and a set of caste rules, and in a
few years appears as a fully equipped member of this great
body. Even Christianity might be welcomed to its wide
embrace, did not the system of caste offer a fatal obstacle,

In attacking caste the Christian is consciously undermining the foundations of native society and religion.

It is in view of these facts that the present introductory chapter forms an indispensable part of this essay. Hinduism presents itself before us in the shape of a highly organized system. Its Law, its Morality, and its Theology are most intimately linked together, having been deduced from the same speculative doctrines, formulated in the same schools, and upheld by the same priestly order. The chief Hindu law-book begins with a chapter on the creation of the world and ends with a chapter on the liberation of the soul. Yet speculative as the doctrine of the books may be, it is far from being entirely disconnected with the life of the people, however divergent the aspect which this presents. It has effected vast transformations in usage and belief in the past, and is implied in every aim which a Hindu sets before himself. It has offered itself as a great ideal, which fact followed, if somewhat tardily, behind. Most of the religion, law, and morality of India is in origin entirely disconnected with the dogmas of the schools; yet in every case the speculation has been attached to the facts and is regarded as their explanation.

What, then, is this great theory which has succeeded in uniting such a vast mass of conflicting customs and beliefs ? *The Theory: Dharma and Caste.* The objects, says the Hindu moralist, towards which the efforts of men are directed are in number four, namely *kāma* or the gratification of desire, *artha* or worldly success, *dharma* or the fulfilment of duty, and *moksha* or the liberation of the soul. Of these the first two are in their nature limitless and outside the pale of morality, while duty and salvation are the watchwords of all ethical and religious discourse.

It is around the idea of *dharma*, which we have translated 'duty,' that the thought of India has chiefly loved to play. With this idea is associated all that is noblest, most tender, and most exalted in its literature. It is the conception which has most vitally worked in its history. The great poem, the *Mahābhārata*, is devoted to the glorification of *dharma*, and one of the chief heroes, *Yudhishthira*, is its

1—2

embodiment. The national epic, the *Rāmāyaṇa*, rhapsodized year by year with endless modifications in half the villages of India, is a story of duty and resignation. The basis and defence of caste, the sanction of morality, the hope of salvation, the law of *dharma* is seen in every action, and felt in every experience, great or small.

Actions are good and evil, in neither case fruitless. The unseen law of Fate (*Adṛshṭa*) has from eternity assigned to each its appropriate reward or punishment, in pleasure and pain. Each soul, until it has reaped the fruit of all its evil acts in pain and of all its good acts in pleasure, must pass from birth to birth, now sinking into stocks, trees, stones, or loathsome animals, now rising to the state of a Brahman or a god, at one time suffering torment in hell, and at another enjoying bliss in heaven. This supreme law of good is *dharma.*

Applica-
tion to
Society.

Naturally it is in its application to mankind that this conception first assumes importance, and in this sphere its influence is all-powerful and omnipresent. Custom of family, locality, and caste, law, civil, political, and criminal, worship and ceremonial, all these are included in its scope, and all are supported by its sanction. A kind of intuitionism carried to an extreme is here seen setting the seal of divine legislation even to the most trivial actions, so that, when the word of the Law[1] proclaims as the guides of moral conduct the Veda, the sacred tradition, the customs of virtuous men, and one's own pleasure, the last item is rather added for completeness than as leaving much opening for individual choice. Custom, immemorial custom, is thus to the Hindu a part, and often the whole, of his religion; and conversely the whole framework of society is conceived of as resting on a religious basis. Caste is according to him no institution of human invention. As the Creator divided living creatures into plants and animals, so he divided men into four different castes, and assigned to each its special functions, to the *Brāhman* the pursuit of knowledge and the performance of ceremonial, to the *Kshatriya* the protection of the people, to

[1] Manu ii. 12.

the *Vaiśya* the operations of trade and agriculture, and to the *Śūdra* the service of the other three. As these distinctions are not conventional, so they are unalterable, and as they are based on the nature of things, so they should afford ground neither to pride in the superior nor to shame in the inferior. At this day the village washerman or scavenger is as proud of his occupation as if he were the highest Brāhman in the land[1].

The theory of caste finds its necessary complement in the belief in transmigration. It is not in human nature to endure a position of inferiority without hope of advancement in this life, unless the deeds of a past existence explain men's sufferings and the prospect of a future existence offer a solace. Accordingly metempsychosis is the fundamental article of Hindu faith. It does not indeed appear in the Rg-Veda, and its origin in India is surrounded with obscurity. But not one of the innumerable religious movements which have originated there during twenty-five centuries has failed to assume, and indeed to be based upon, this same doctrine. Every Hindu sets down his joys and misfortunes to the account of his good and evil actions in previous births. He looks forward in some future birth not merely to the state of a Brāhman or a king, but to a sojourn for millions of years in heavens vividly conceived and even to the throne of a deity. From these exalted stations he will not sink down again until the measure of his enjoyment has equalled that of his merits.

Transmigration.

Caste and Transmigration are the two foundations of Hinduism. But a faith which provided no scope for feelings of devotion and reverence needed a superstructure. Nor was such at any period wanting. There was a time when the Aryans as we know them from the Rg-Veda looked forward to no state beyond a life on earth, or had only the vaguest glimpses of a Hades ruled by Yama, king of the dead. From the gods, chiefly deified natural powers, whom they worshipped, they asked only such mundane goods as they could conceive, health, victory over enemies, and riches

Liberation of the Soul.

[1] Compare Sleeman, *Rambles of an Indian Official,* I. 64—5.

in cattle, horses, grain, and land. Gradually in the hands of a priesthood sacrifice and worship came to be regarded as a mere mechanical device for extorting these blessings from the gods. Thence arose a mass of formulae which the pharisees of all religions might envy. The business of worship must be transacted without the smallest error in detail, or its effect was vitiated. Every conceivable variety of mistake must be provided for; and when all perceptible informalities had been removed, priests had to be stationed muttering charms as an antidote to such as were beyond sense and calculation. This is the theory of the sacrifice, in its very completeness characteristically philosophical, which still remains an integral part of native religion.

Meanwhile the spiritual life of the people was to be found elsewhere. When religion had been swallowed up in formulae, philosophy arose to take its place. When the priests had reduced the scene of sacrifice to an exhibition of ceremonial, there had grown up among men of the caste of nobles a custom of fleeing away to communicate with their own souls in the woods. The fashion was followed by Brahmans, and the spirit which dictated the movement was not long unfruitful. Among these men there arose two systems of philosophy which have played a great part in the development of Indian religion. The first, the dualistic or _Sāṅkhya_ philosophy, to which Buddhism bears certain affinities, and which has greatly influenced the thought of the _Vaishṇava_ sects, admits of two principles, matter and the individual soul. It was only later that it consented to the supposition of a God. The second, or _Vedānta_ system, incomparably the more important of the two, is severely monistic. Asserting the identity of the individual soul with God, it regards the phenomenal world as the result of illusion or ignorance, the removal of which leaves only one single essence which is soul or God, and which can be defined, though only conventionally, as 'existence, knowledge, and joy.' But both these systems, differing as they do, the one atheistic, the other pantheistic, the one asserting two principles, the other having 'Advaita' or 'non-duality'

for its watchword, were in their bearings on practical religion and morality entirely at one. Both seek the same
end, and both inculcate the same means, namely the pursuit
of knowledge. Examine nature through and through, says
the *Sāṅkhya*, and thereby escape from her bondage.

'As a dancer, having exhibited herself on the stage, ceases to dance,
'So does Nature cease when she has made herself manifest to soul.
....
'Nothing is more modest than Nature ; that is my judgment.
'Saying 'I have been seen' she does not expose herself again to the
     view of soul[1].'

Examine nature through and through, says the Vedānta,
that realizing her unreality the soul may sink back into
itself and regain—what indeed it has never lost—its unity
with God. Here then we are in contact with something
fundamental. The Hindu is cheerful, but his cheerfulness is
based on a deep-rooted pessimism. Belonging to a tropical
race he has but little taste for the pleasure of active and
vigorous exertion. He conceives of life as pain, and even in
the most absorbing pleasure he has a sense of limitation
and finitude. His deepest aspiration has always been to
escape from a world of pain and iron necessity, whether he
defines his end with the Buddhist as annihilation, with the
Sāṅkhya philosopher as independent existence, or with the
Vedantist as union with God. To this end the sacred law
has arranged the whole scheme of the life of the twice-born.
The first period is to be spent in the acquirement of learning. Next come marriage and the daily life of the householder. But 'when a householder sees his skin wrinkled
and his hair white, and the sons of his sons, then he may
resort to the forest[2]' there to communicate with his soul
and fix his thoughts on God. Lastly, when he has freed
himself from every trace of earthly emotion or desire, he may
return to live an uninterested spectator of the fortunes of
his kindred. Liberation, then, by knowledge forms the second
grand element in Hindu religion.

---

[1] Sāṅkhya-Kārikā of Iṣvara-Kṛṣhṇa (trans. Davies).
[2] Manu VI. 2.

Devotion to God.   But neither the doctrine of works, assigning to each act of duty and worship and to each degree of austerity its fixed reward, nor the doctrine of liberation by knowledge, nor even the union of the two, suffice for the framework of a living religion. For two thousand years the ruling thought of religious India has been neither of these doctrines, but rather the conception of ' *bhakti* ' or devotion to God. Every Hindu admits and acts upon the belief in the inexorable law of Dharma. Every instructed Hindu, to whatever sect he belongs, accepts in the end the theory of the world-illusion and the identity of the soul with Brahma. But the feeling which has dictated the lavish prodigality, toilsome pilgrimages, and terrible austerities characteristic of native piety has been devotion, whether to Vishṇu in his various incarnations or the many 'forms' of Ṣiva. Beside the form-less Brahma the ancient Brāhmanism conceived of a trinity of Gods, Brahmā, Vishṇu and Ṣiva, presiding respectively over the creation, maintenance, and destruction of the world. Of the personal devotion of Hinduism Brahmā has reaped but little: Vishṇu and Ṣiva, and by the side of each their personified powers conceived of as female goddesses have the enjoyment of it in full measure. According as he chooses Vishṇu, Ṣiva, or their 'powers' as the chief object of his devotion, every individual is a Vaishṇava, a Ṣaiva, or a Ṣāktā, and these divisions, which however neither in theory nor in fact are mutually exclusive, together embrace the whole of the community.

To what end, it will now be asked, is this devotion di-rected? The answer reveals one of the contradictions which abound in native theology. The devotion of the several sects has raised each god in turn above his fellows and identified him with the primitive essence Brahma, thereby giving rise to great confusion and some unorthodox meta-physics. The personality of Vishṇu or Ṣiva is too vivid for them to be conceived as absolute unqualified being, and hence in connection with these gods a dualistic conception has gained ground, substituting for absorption a kind of mystical approximation to the deity. Thus while the path of 'bhakti,' like that of jñāna or knowledge, is directed towards the liberation of the soul, the end is here conceived rather more vividly as a resting on god and a dwelling in an everlasting heaven. In all this we recognize on the one hand the influence of the later or theistic Sānkhya philosophy and on the other the 'aberglaube' necessary to a popular religion. But it should not be forgotten that the orthodox Hindu while regarding these conceptions as true from a certain point of view, returns at all times to the Vedānta conception of non-duality as the full and final expression of the whole truth.

Such in necessarily brief and imperfect outline is the *Remarks on the system.* theory of Hinduism. I hope that it has been made clear that the system, while culminating in a mystic philosophy, has its roots in the everyday life and thought of the people. To criticise it or to point out its obvious defects is not part of our present purpose. But three points demand a brief consideration, namely, the age of the system, its relation to government, and its relation to the stranger.

The whole theory here described has existed for at least 1. *Its age.* fifteen-hundred years in as complete a form as at present. Were we to omit the notion of 'bhakti,' we might substitute for fifteen, as many as twenty-five, centuries. Devotion to chosen gods and demigods, such as Vishṇu, Rāma, and Kṛeshṇa was the lever whereby Brāhmanism sought to expel the long dominant Buddhism from its midst. Its success, completed in the eighth century of our era, converted what had long been one of the chief realia of native religion into an ineradicable element of its doctrine, and the conception became fixed as a vital part of one coherent system at least two centuries before the Muhammadan conquest began in earnest under the great Mahmud of Ghazni.

The separation of Church and State is a western develop- 2. *Its relation to government.* ment of late date, to which the East has never attained, least of all in India. A religion which claimed to be nothing less than a complete expression of divine law and truth could not regard government as more than an agency for enforcing a part of its ordinances. It tied down the king to the advice of the commentator and theologian. It assigned to every part of the state its proper functions, to transgress which was not only a crime but a sin. Yet according to the same primitive conception found in all undeveloped societies, the king was held to rule by divine right and to be in a sense a god; and it is easy to see that within a certain sphere everything must have depended on his individual character. A 'good' king would obey the law himself and compel his subjects to follow his example, while a 'bad' one would neglect the advice of his Brāhman minister and follow his own depraved judgment. In this case the system, being devoid of any special sanction and in no case recognising a right to rebel[1], was left to defend itself. Strong in the unquestioning belief and usage of the people, appealing directly to the conscience of the king himself, it might be temporarily disregarded in part and set aside, but after a while it would be seen in operation as vigorous as before administering penance to repentant sinners. Paraṣu-Rāma, the mythical Brāhman hero, is said to have cleared the earth twenty-one times of the Kshatriya race, and the story, as has been said, contains a kernel of truth. Even if the sinner were prosperous in this life, there was the ready consolation that the outraged law would in another birth, at any rate, avenge itself on those who had neglected it.

3. *Its relation to the stranger.* By the Catholic religions, Muhammadanism and Christianity, and to a certain extent Buddhism as well, the stranger is regarded as a soul to be saved by acquaintance with the truth. But what could Hinduism, with its peculiar theories attached to an unique society have to say to the foreigner, whose existence it had not originally contemplated? The Hebrew could at least regard other nations as the enemies of his race and of Jehovah; but to the Hindu this was from the nature of his philosophical doctrines impossible. In a pantheistic religion the chosen people embraces all mankind. The ingenuity of Brāhmanism has however sufficed to provide a solution of this difficult problem. This is the fourth and worst age of the world. The four original castes, which

[1] 'Whatever a king does is right, that is a settled rule,' Nārada xviii. 21.

in early and purer times included the whole of mankind, have now been infinitely confounded by intermarriage. Thus have arisen the mixed castes, of higher or lower degree according as they diverge less or more from the original divisions and customs allotted by the Creator. Lowest of all in the scale, as belonging to no ascertainable caste and retaining no trace of Brahmanical institutions, stand the ' *Mlecchas* ' or foreigners, whose genealogy is of dreadful complication, and whom in this life no degree of virtue can elevate to the rank of the humblest pariah in the land of Bhārata. In this culminating fiction Hinduism signed its own death-warrant. The day was inevitably to come when the Hindu would have to recognize not only power but also worth in the foreigner; and then the system was destined to fall *en masse* as a system of belief, however large a proportion of its usages and institutions could maintain its ground. In another hundred years it will probably live only in the dreams of a few isolated Brahmans. How many of its beliefs will survive in another form is a matter on which something will be said in a later chapter.

It happened by a strange chance that the first foreign power with which the natives of India were brought into permanent contact was one differing as widely as possible in derivation, in manners and in religion, but chiefly the last. Muhammadanism is in most respects the very antithesis of Hinduism. While the latter is a huge aggregate imperfectly compacted together in the course of many centuries, the former was the creation of a single mind, and is expressed in a single sentence 'there is one God, and Muhammad is his prophet.' Hinduism is melancholy, sentimental, and philosophical; Muhammadanism is ardent, austere, and practical. The former has for its basis the wish to escape from the limitations of the world, the latter abhorrence of sin and hope of heaven. While the latter detests idolatry beyond all other sins, the former has encouraged or permitted the worship of every creation, animate or inanimate, human or divine. Lastly, while the Hindu has consecrated innumerable humiliating distinctions among men, all true believers, whatever their origin or previous life, are admitted by the Mu-

Muhammadanism contrasted with Hinduism.

hammadan, if only in theory, to a social and religious equality [1].

Charac-
teristics of
Muham-
madanism.
The Arabian prophet came forward as a restorer, not as an innovator, as the vehicle of a revelation, yet not of a new one. The primitive and only true religion, a pure monotheism, was, he asserted, constantly overlaid with idolatry and corruption, until it was periodically restored by the burning zeal of prophets sent by God [2]. Of this great chain, proceeding from Adam through Noah and Moses to Christ, he claimed to be the final link. His mission was indeed akin both in its character and aim to that of the Hebrew prophets, but with one great difference. The Hebrew prophets had come to restore Israel: Mahomet, inspired by the spectacle of universal Christianity, addressed his commission to the whole world. Thus in Muhammadanism, as in Christianity, the Semite opens the treasury of his truth to all nations. But whereas Christianity had quickly divested itself of the narrow bigotry of Judaism and winning its way by the persuasive appeals of reason to the individual conscience had established a world-wide society with other laws than Caesar's, Mahomet was the founder at once of a faith and a nation. A race of enthusiasts, he inspired the Arabs with the idea of purifying the beliefs of mankind: a nation of robbers, he opened out to them the prospect of plundering a world. The double aspect of this vast conception characterizes the whole history of Islam. The Sultans and their janissaries were in a sense the genuine successors of Mahomet and his warrior saints.

Islam, therefore, unlike Hinduism, was an essentially expansive religion. A share in its Paradise was offered to all. It hurled itself upon the world bidding it choose between conversion, subjection, and the sword. And certainly its claim to universal sovereignty was nearly successful. Before his death the prophet saw himself master of Arabia and had already begun to assail his neighbours. Four years later in 636 A.D. the power of Persia was shattered at the battle of

---

[1] 'In Islam all men are alike' is a speech of the Khalif Omar, quoted by Muir, *Annals of the Early Khalifate*,' p. 203.

[2] Quran II. 212, III. 19, and, concerning Prophets, *passim*.

Kadisiya, and when the last Sassanian died in 651 A.D. the Oxus separated the Musalman from the Turk. A century from the Hijra the northern frontier had been advanced to the Jaxartes and the conquest of Sindh had brought Islam into contact with Hinduism. In the west Alexandria fell in 640, Antioch in 638; Carthage was torn from the Empire sixty years later, Spain invaded in 710, and the triumphant advance of Islam was checked only when it met the young vigour of the West under Charles Martel on the momentous field of Tours.

Meanwhile, the faith which inspired this wonderful activity was being formulated in dogma. These concern first of all the sources of the faith, the Qurān and the Tradition, secondly their contents, and thirdly the Khalifate and Imamate, law and society. On each of these topics it is necessary to touch briefly. But first a word concerning the general aspects of Islam.

Uniformity and fixity are generally held to be the chief characteristics of Muhammadanism. Arrogant and intolerant, it everywhere enunciates the same dogmas, prescribes the same laws, upholds the same constitution, and follows the same custom. It is to-day the great barrier to the progress of the world. Each of these statements contains a truth. Yet in almost every case the opposite either is or has in the past been in some measure true. Uniform as its aspect is, perhaps there is no faith which has to such a degree taken the character of the peoples who have accepted it. At Constantinople it is not the same as at Mecca: in Persia it has followed its strangest development: in India it has been deeply imbued with native superstitions. Its apparent originality might seem to be entirely fictitious. It has been indebted to almost every religion. Its dogmatism and asceticism is borrowed from Christianity, its mysticism from India and Alexandria, its philosophy from Greece: the idea of a Messiah came direct from Judaism[1]. 'Its culture is nothing but an agglomerate of borrowings

---

[1] A. van Kremer, *Culturgeschichtliche Streifzüge auf dem Gebiete des Islam*, p. 54.

from the peoples whom the Arabs overthrew with such astonishing rapidity[1].' On the other hand, it has not always been an intolerant religion. On the contrary, it was during the middle ages as conspicuously superior in this respect as it was in point of liberality and culture. Its intolerance dates from the time of its decay. With the downfall of the Khalifate, perished at once its free spirit and its civilisation. Scholastic theology destroyed rationalism with its own weapons, and Islam thus entered upon that sleep which has lasted for five centuries till now[2]. Yet Muhammadanism has never practised systematic persecution, and more than one writer has accused it of an even excessive tolerance. The tolerance of the Afghans has been commented upon, and according to a distinguished scholar and traveller[3] there is no land where free thought is so little interfered with as in Persia. So far as Islam is intolerant this is due to the spirit of its now dominant orthodoxy, and so far as it cherishes a fanatic hatred against Christian Europe, this is due to fear and to resentment for its losses[4].

The reconciliation of these antitheses is not, however, impossible. Islam is uniform because it is little beside formula. Amid every variety of belief its creed, its five daily prayers, its practice of pilgrimage remain the same. It offers no high moral ideal, it exercises no deep moral influence. Beliefs and morals change, but to his creeds and formulas the Muhammadan holds with all the greater tenacity the less he believes and understands. But it must not be thought in spite of all that these formulae are quite dead and meaningless. They are the symbol of the influence of Mahomet and the Arab race. Whatever is living or capable of revivification in Muhammadanism is the spirit and life of the prophet. Islam, however varied its aspect, bears this ineffaceable stamp, and whenever a revival is attempted the forms regain their meaning, but they are never abolished.

---

[1] Vambéry, *Der Islam im 19 ten Jahrhundert*, p. 61.
[2] Vambéry, *Ibid.* p. 67.
[3] Vambéry, *Ibid.* p. 32, 3.
[4] Vambéry, *Ibid.* p. 280.

Secondly, Muhammadanism is intolerant of change. But this is because it is a system as well as a religion. The outlines of its social constitution are enjoined or implied in the Quran itself, and to change them is to impair the very authority of the founder. This is the fatal defect of the religion. It has barred its progress and the barrier can never be removed. It has even erred on the side of defect: for the theoretically elective character of the Khalifs and their successors has given occasion, as in the case of the Roman emperors, to endless bloodshed and disorder. Thirdly, Muhammadanism is intolerant as being a zealot religion. The ordinance of warring against the unbeliever lays it under the necessity either of subduing or of being subdued. Where strong it is bound to be aggressive, and it can only be held in check by fear. On the other hand it has adopted the first part of Vergil's admonition to his Romans 'parcere subjectis et debellare superbos,' and its subjects experience apart from occasional outbreaks on the whole no intolerable yoke.

Islam rests on a fourfold foundation, the Qurān, the *Hadis* or tradition, the *Ijmā* or concurrence of the learned, and *Qiyās* or analogical reasoning. The Qurān, the text of which was fixed under the Khalif Osman about thirty years after the Hijra, is the word of God revealed through his prophet. There is no syllable of it that is not due to the direct inspiration of the Creator. Nay, the dogma, once persecuted under the Khalif Mamun (A.H. 218), has since the third century been universally held by Sunni Muhammadans[1] that the book is even prior to creation, being eternally present in the mind of God. This, the most logical of all theories of inspiration, bears a close resemblance to the Hindu theory of the eternity of the Veda, which the great sages are said not to have indited, but to have *seen* before the beginning of the world. The *tradition* of the companions of the prophet arose to supply the deficiencies of the Qurān when the expansion of the empire had opened new questions and difficulties which could not present them-

1. The foundations of the faith.

[1] *v.* Hughes, *Dict. of Islam,* p. 521; *Encycl. Brit.* xvi. p. 606.

selves within the confines of Arabia. When the Qurān was
in vain explored for guidance, recourse was had to the
sayings and acts of Mahomet as recorded by those who lived
with him and handed down in unbroken succession. The
traditions, which it will be seen have a definiteness and
historical appearance characteristically Semitic and which
bear no resemblance to the Christian tradition of the Church,
were ultimately collected and formed into digests. A vast
number of them are admittedly and a still greater number
actually unauthentic[1], and the collections of the Shiahs,
which differ entirely from those of the Sunnis, have been
described as a pack of forgeries[2]. The *Ijmā* or consensus of
the learned holds a place in some degree corresponding to
the decisions of the Church Councils, while *Qiyās* consists of
reasoning on the analogy of the Qurān and the words and
acts of Mahomet. *Ijmā* is generally held by the Sunnis to
be no longer possible, owing to the divisions and sects in
Islam, but among the Shiahs in Persia it is still collected
and accepted[3].

The relative authority of the four foundations of the
faith has been accurately defined in detail by the learning of
the theologians. In practical matters the Hadiṣ and the
Ijmā are of great importance, and guide the *fatwās* or legal
decisions of the *Ulemās*, the judges and juris consulti of
Muhammadan states. But none of the three approaches in
any way to the authority of the Qurān. The masterpiece of
style, the very word of God, the sacred volume dominates
the whole horizon of Islam. Every Musalman knows a
portion of it by heart or at least by rote; a verse oppor-
tunely quoted may save a life or lose one, may cause or
check a revolution, found or confound the claims of a Mahdi.
Too definite, too full to encourage plausible explanation by
way of symbolism and allegory it has condemned the religion to a fixity and sterility which must remain with it to
the end.

---

[1] Vide Muir's discussion in his *Life of Mahomet*.
[2] *Encycl. Brit.* Art. *Sunni*, xxii. p. 664, n. 2.
[3] *Dict. Islam*, p. 197.

Muhammadanism is the least mystical of religions. It pro- 2. *The* *Doctrines* claims certain doctrines and enjoins certain observances. But *of Islam.* to explain the world, to elucidate the relation of the soul thereto and to the Creator, are enquiries towards which it has not evinced any great disposition. Great philosophers and rationalistic sects have arisen in its midst. But the faith is neither metaphysical itself nor has it—with one great exception—evoked metaphysical interpretation. There is nothing in orthodox Muhammadanism analogous to the Christian controversy concerning Homoousia and Homoi-ousia.

The six articles of the Musalman creed are the Unity of God, Angels, the Qurān, the Prophets, the Day of Judgment, and Predestination, while the recitation of the *Kalma* or creed, the five daily prayers, the fast during the month Ramadan, the payment of alms, and the pilgrimage to Mecca form the five pillars of its practice. None of these require to be discussed here. Only it should be emphasized that absolute predestination is a dogma inculcated in the Qurān and accepted by all orthodox Musalmans[1]. The Khalif Omar threatened with death a Christian priest who denied that God foreordains the evil actions of the wicked as well as the good actions of the good. The enlightened Motazalite sect, which amid other great services to culture fought against the orthodox fatalism and anthropomorphism[2], fell, after a period of prevalence during the golden age of Islam, before the weapons of scholasticism.

Yet Muhammadanism contains a germ of mysticism, 3. *The* *Khalifate,* namely in its theory of inspiration: and this germ has *Law, and* grown to great dimensions and been at the root of most of *Society.* the sectarian divisions amongst Musalmans. The prophet was the religious and political guide of his followers. To provide successors to his worldly power might be a simple matter: his spiritual heirs must possess special titles. Ma-

[1] Quran xiv. 4, 'God misleadeth whom he will, and whom he will he guideth.' xvii. 14, 'The fate of every man have we bound about his neck.'

[2] *Dict. Islam,* pp. 425, 472 sqq.; Sale's *Preliminary Discourse* (Wherry), pp. 242—3; Kremer, *Culturgeschichte,* ii. pp. 45, 413.

T. 2

homet himself had enjoined the appointment of a successor,
to be elected by the faithful, but had neither restricted the
office to any special group or family nor, apart from pro-
hibiting a division of the faith[1], had he laid down any rules
to guide the choice. Accordingly three main dogmas have
been upheld, that of the *Kharijites* or extreme puritan and
democratic party, which regarded every Musalman as eligible,
that of the *Shiahs*, which restricts the succession to Mahomet's descendants through Fatima his daughter and her
husband Ali, and the orthodox view which confines it to the
Quraish, the Meccan tribe from which Mahomet sprung.
Both the Kharijites and the Sunnis might find some support
in Muhammad's policy towards his family and his followers;
but the Shiah view partakes of the mendacious character of
Shiahism in general. The fourth party, that of the Abbasides, which held the Khalifate during the most brilliant era
of Islam, rose to power by the support of the Shiahs and
then kicked away the ladder by which it had risen. It
assigns the succession to the descendants of the prophet's
uncle Abbas. Of these four sects only the Sunnis and the
Shiahs retain any great importance. At the present day
Shiahism is found only in Persia, where it is the orthodox
faith, and in certain districts of India: the remainder of the
Musalman world is Sunni.

In the East, however, it is not right but force which
commonly forms the basis of sovereignty, and but few of the
Khalifs had any real title[2] to their office. Even the Sunnis,
who are able to recognize the legitimacy of the succession
down to the arrival of the Turks, are compelled to draw a
distinction between the first four 'well-directed' Khalifs[3],
who were lawfully elected, and the succeeding Umayyads
and Abbasides under whom the hereditary principle prevailed. The present Sultan of Turkey has no claim which
is not based upon fiction. The Shiahs recognize a succession
of twelve, Ali and eleven of his descendants, whom they

---

[1] According to a tradition: *v. Dict. Islam*, p. 266.

[2] *i.e.* based on a genuine election.

[3] *v. Dict. Islam*, p. 264.

prefer to entitle *imāms* and of whom only the first was ever head of Islam. The last of them, the concealed Imam, they claim to have been rapt away from the world during his lifetime, to return again as the Imam Mahdi to restore the faith. And here it should be pointed out that the theory of the twelve Imams involves Aryan and pagan conceptions which the Persians have introduced into a faith imposed upon them by force. One important Shiah sect, that of the Ismailiyas[1], which recognizes in part a special line of Imams, regards Ali and his successors as incarnations of God; and, though the orthodox Shiahs in theory stop short of this, yet this conception is everywhere implied, and Ali and his sons Haçan and Huçain commonly receive greater honours even than the prophet himself. In fact, Persia was never really converted to Islam, and if there is any real religious sentiment existing among the Persians—which has been doubted—it gathers round this half-pagan, half-philosophical and Buddhist notion of the incarnation of God in a succession of men. Concerning the Ṣufi philosophy, which though found throughout Islam, yet had its origin in Indian ideas naturalized in Persia, something will be said below[2].

The authority of the Khalif reigns in every department of religion and government[3]. It is his duty to learn the prayers as *imām* in the mosque, he is the supreme legislator, administrator, general, and judge. But he can delegate each of these powers to fit subordinates, and on this theory of delegation the whole Musalman system is founded. In the first place, the Khalif may delegate his imperial powers in a limited or unlimited measure to his minister, and thus occupy towards him the position either of a master or of a slave. In the most flourishing times of Islam the Khalifs kept their ministers well in check, controlled their appointments, and set a limit to their influence: but at the end of

---

[1] On their tenets, v. *Encycl. Brit.* ii. 722, xvi. 593, Sale's *Discourse* (Wherry), p. 278, and Malcolm's *Persia*, i. 240.

[2] Chap. iii.

[3] On the position of the Khalif, &c., the best authority is Kremer, *op. cit.* esp. i. cc. v. and viii.

the Abbaside period the Persian Buyides had come to occupy quite the position of the *majores domus* of the Merovingian emperors, while the Khalif, reft of his worldly power, retained only the spiritual consideration due to the successor of Mahomet[1]. The same history has been repeated again and again wherever Muhammadanism has ruled, not least in India, and the Sultan is everywhere a despot or a dependent according to the strength or weakness of his individual character. In the East there is in such matters no *via media*. Secondly, the Khalif may delegate a less or greater degree of authority to his provincial governors. In the former case their appointment rests on his firman, their powers are limited to general superintendence, they forward to the central government whatever revenue remains over and above the cost of administration, and they may be dismissed for misconduct. In the second case, they exercise within their province all the functions of the Khalif, appointing judges, and muftis, regulating taxation, and forwarding either nothing at all or a fixed tribute to their overlord: they commonly appoint their successors, and naturally in their own family, while the firman becomes a mere recognition of the *status quo*. This is the process whereby great empires in the East break up and go to pieces, the satrap quickly assuming the power and not seldom the name of king: a process which has nowhere prevailed to a greater extent than in Muhammadanism. Thirdly, the Khalif delegates his priestly offices to the *imāms* or leaders of prayer in the temple, though on his accession it is his duty to preach a coronation sermon to the assembled Musalmans. Fourthly, the Kazi represents the judicial authority of the Khalif, who exercises jurisdiction at the most only in cases of appeal. Nor must we in this place omit to mention that body of men, who under the title of *ulemas* represent the democratic element and the second power in Islam. The qualifications for each of the offices of state are accurately defined by the theoretical laws and theology. The Kazi is appointed from

[1] Cf. *Encycl. Brit.* xvi. 587, xxiii. 661, Kremer, *Culturgeschichte &c.*, i. 185, 396, and Malcolm's *Persia*, i. 158.

among the *élèves* of the schools, and on matters of doubt it is their duty to defer to the decisions of the doctors. So elaborate is the theoretical law of Islam, such consequently the solidarity among the body of the learned, such influence has it with the people at large, that the learned form a corporation which constitutes a formidable check on the despotism of the most resolute princes and has not seldom sufficed to overthrow it. Whether in Persia or in Turkey the chief Mufti or Mollah is conscious of wielding a most real influence in the state, an influence only lessened by the universal venality of Musalman officers of law. The Ulemas, from the bigotry and fanatic ignorance of all but their special subject which prevails among them, form one of the great barriers to progress[1].

Concerning the actual law of Islam so much only need be said, that among the Sunnis four schools are recognized as orthodox, and that the most liberal of the four, the Hanafite school, which admits the principle of reason, was that to which the Afghan conquerors of Hindustan belonged. As concerns social institutions, that Islam favours despotism and also in a measure democracy[2], whence it has always been hostile to the growth of a middle class and the institutions and sentiments which this fosters: that it has sanctioned polygamy, though the vast majority of Musalmans has always been from poverty monogamous: and that, while it has endeavoured to lay down rules for the mitigation of slavery, it has never aimed at a final extirpation of that pest.

Such was the framework of the society which the conquests of Mahmud of Ghazni brought into contact with Hinduism. The spirit of the two civilisations and of the races which had created them was essentially opposed. But it is impossible to overlook certain resemblances. Both were theocratic in character, recognizing in their inspired books a guide to life as well as to faith. Both had conse- *Possibility of interaction between the two systems.*

---

[1] On the Ulemas, *v. Encycl. Brit.* **xxii.** 660—2, Art. *Sunni*; *Dict. Islam*, p. 650; Malcolm's *Persia*, **ii.** 304 and 311—320.

[2] Represented by the Ulemas, *v. supra.*

quently developed in great detail their academic theories of government and its duties, and in both cases the actual presented vast divergences from the ideal. In both religions the lawyers and doctors exercised an extraordinary influence. The Muhammadan land system, borrowed in a large measure from Persia, has points of resemblance with that of the Hindus, and even the peculiar institution of the Post has a parallel in the Hindu system of espionage. But while such resemblances are undeniable, yet they are of little importance when compared with still more fundamental differences; and so far were they from encouraging any fusion between the two religions in India that their influence may be said to have tended in the opposite direction. When Islam was introduced into India, both systems had long settled down into permanent grooves. The most important Musalman sects had already taken shape, the sources of Law had long been finally settled, and every school, whether of law or of dogma, was fully equipped with authorities, texts and commentaries. Among the Hindus this was even more exclusively the case, inasmuch as Hinduism had displayed a longer, more peaceful, and more concentrated activity. Add to this that it was not the Shiahs, who had already felt the influence of Hindu speculation in Persia, and who represented the more adaptable part of Muhammadanism, that won and governed India, but a branch, if the least illiberal branch, of the orthodox Sunnis.

In what manner then could the two systems exercise any wide-reaching influence? Only indirectly. The sharp contrasts of theory could be toned down, if at all, only in consequence of the interaction of facts. Hinduism and Muhammadanism could exercise mutual influence only through the intercommunion of Hindus and Musalmans. To seek in the orthodox books of the two religions for traces of intermixture would be not only fruitless, but *a limine* mistaken, since these books were either written before the two peoples came into contact, or are repetitions, commentaries, and deductions, attached to such books. On the other hand, if we once desert the high road of theory, we might seem to be landed in a wilderness of divergent and disconnected facts but imperfectly ascertained. Apart from Hinduism and Muhammadanism we know but little concerning the Hindus at any rate. To this we can only reply, firstly, that the scholastic and theological theories in question are not so entirely at variance with the facts that these fail to shed light on one another; in the second place, that the facts themselves are not so chaotic as might be supposed. The interaction of Hindus and Muhammadans is a stage in a great development, which has been going on since the first dawn of Indian history, and has still to be completed, from multiformity and chaos to unity and order. In the process, which is destined to consolidate the various tribes and nations of India into a single people, the Muhammadan empire has played a great part. Imperfectly and rudely as this was accomplished, we must remember that by recognising a single emperor at Agra or Delhi, by professing throughout India a religion which at any rate bore a single name and enunciated a single system of law and morality, by breaking down divisions between tribes, races, and territories, Muhammadanism has prepared the way for an unification which the great Akbar conceived, which his wide rule foreshadowed, and which it is the mission of the English, mediately or immediately, to complete. It is in the light of this development that the Musalman rule becomes, if very imperfectly, intelligible.

CHAPTER I.

MUTUAL INFLUENCE OF HINDUS AND MUHAMMADANS IN GOVERNMENT, LAND TENURE, AND LAW.

Pre-Mu-hammadan India: Government. UNDER its native rulers India, like ancient Greece, was a country of small principalities. Occasionally, it is true, powerful empires arose and held out for a time. But from the tendency of all subordinate offices to become hereditary, from the practice here and there followed of partition of kingdoms at the king's death[1], and from other causes, every considerable kingdom was quickly dissolved by division. In fact, even to the end of the Hindu period government was still in a state of transition. The Aryans who invaded India, though closely connected by blood, language, and culture, were minutely divided into tribes and families, and they followed each other in successive waves. They conquered the country at first by driving one part of the original inhabitants southwards, seizing their land, and reducing those who remained to a state of servitude. In this manner the larger part of Hindustan would be won. But there was a second and more peaceful method, which had cooperated even north of the Vindhya range, but which was probably of the first importance in the later appropriation of the Dekhan. The Brahmanical hermitages preceded the armies of the Kshatriyas, or indeed replaced them. Peacefully settling, as Englishmen have done in later times, among

---

[1] A case is quoted by Baden-Powell, *Land System of British India*, p. 57.

the wild tribes, these missionaries succeeded very largely in introducing their institutions and laws, a process which has not ceased even at the present day. When a tribe was sufficiently advanced, the missionary would not be long in discovering in its rulers a branch of the warrior race, in its cultivators the descendants of a Vaiṣya family, and in its serfs or inferior classes, if such existed, a body of the despised Ṣudras; while if the tribe was too wild to exhibit any such divisions these were soon partially introduced. The Brahmans themselves would represent the fourth, or priestly caste, and in a few years, the tribe would assume the aspect of a branch of the Brahmanical society. Polyandry and human sacrifice would tend to disappear along with cannibalism and the nomadic life. In short, what Muhammadanism is doing at this day for northern and central Africa, that Brahmanism did for the Dekhan and parts of Hindustan in the first few centuries before and after Christ. The assimilation was never more than partial, but the general outlines of the sacred order were everywhere introduced.

The conquest of India was then achieved in part by the military superiority of a group of Aryan tribes acting under a common impulse but without a common organisation, in part through a process of assimilation due to the independent efforts of the missionaries of a system. Hence the subdivision of the country into small kingdoms[1]. They represent a stage in a process which was advancing throughout the Hindu period, and which was rudely hurried forward under the Muhammadans. Whether India, if left to itself, would have advanced more or less rapidly in this direction, is an interesting question which can scarcely be settled. Was the character of its people too unenterprizing, were their habits of thought too fixed, their differences of race and culture too pronounced, to be removed, if at all, by anything but a common oppression? To these queries no safe reply can be given. We can only point to the fact that no strictly Hindu power ever has held together, but

---

[1] Hiuen-Thsang gives us descriptions of no less than eighty, some of them, it is true, dependent on others.

each mass in turn has solidified about a number of different centres.

But, though even at the end of the Hindu period political unity was thus conspicuously absent, yet the type of government and society was almost universally the same. There was a substantial resemblance in three most important departments, in land tenure and the general framework of society, in the character of the law, and in religion. In what sense this is true of the last will be discussed later. The first two topics will engage us immediately.

The village and its constitution. Every scientific treatment of Hindu law and government must always begin at the bottom and with the unit, inasmuch as all native institutions are essentially local, and society has attained only to a comparatively weak development. The unit is to be found not, as in Modern Europe, in the individual, nor, as in early Greece and Rome, in the family, but in the village. Under the native rulers this must have been everywhere the case, and in the Panjab and the North-west Provinces the British Government still treats not with the individual cultivator but with the village officer. Private ownership in land was never universal. The fields were in many parts periodically redistributed among certain families who possessed the right to cultivate them. Beyond the Indus redistribution is still customary and a dim sense of its legality survives in many parts of India[1]. The corporation in which the right of cultivation was vested and which possessed the exclusive management of the affairs of the village did not embrace the whole population. On the one hand were excluded the low-caste families dwelling on the outskirts of the village, who in return for a customary allowance performed a number of menial offices; on the other hand all such as were required to pay rent for the right to pasture cattle, and to build houses within the village precincts. The former class consisted of the descendants of the conquered aborigines, while the latter were either strangers holding land under the corporation or local

---

[1] *Vide* Boulnois and Rattigan, *Customary Law in the Panjab*, p. 204.

head, or, being permanent occupants, yet lacked the full rights belonging to the original stock.

The land in each village was divided into three portions, the arable land, the pasture land, and the waste, of which the last two were never distributed. The question of rights over the waste introduces us to the distinction which must have existed at least in some measure in Hindu times between two types of villages, which have been named respectively the 'joint' and the 'non-united[1].' They differed in two important respects. In the first place, the cultivators of the 'joint' village claimed to be the descendants of the original founder or conqueror of the village, the whole of which was vested in them as coheirs and for the revenue from which they were jointly responsible to the king: the right to clear and till the waste they regarded as exclusively their own, and none could occupy land within the precincts except as their servants and tenants. In the non-united villages the sense of common origin was less conspicuous than in the case of such as were 'joint,' and the waste was at the disposal of the governor or king. In the second place the two classes of villages differed somewhat in point of government. The joint villages were managed by a 'pancayat' or committee of five, elected from the land-owning families and jointly responsible. But in the second class of villages the management of affairs rested with certain village officers, the headman, the accountant, the watchman, and others. The office of the headman, the most important of these, was partly elective and partly hereditary, and his functions included the distribution of the assessment among the different families, the settlement of disputes, the decision of minor cases, and the arrest of offenders. The accountant kept the village records, containing minute descriptions of boundaries, the character of the soil, terms of occupancy, and the like. The watchman kept guard over the crops, took note of the characters of the inhabitants, and performed the duties of policeman and

---

[1] *Vide* Baden-Powell, *Land Systems of British India, passim,* and esp. pp. 44—76.

messenger. It is needless to proceed with the list. Sufficient has been said to show to what a large extent the non-united as well as the 'joint' village corporations were entrusted with the management of their own affairs, and to demonstrate the principles upon which this internal government was based.

Both the 'joint' and the 'non-united' types of villages existed in Hindu times. The latter, which appears to be that treated of in the early Sanskrit law-books, was the earlier; the former, found chiefly in the North-West, is thought to have come in with the later Jat and Rajput immigration[1]. Important however as the distinction between the two has become, it cannot have been so prominent in Hindu times. For periodic redistribution is known to have been practised in both[2]. The ownership of the joint villages was of less importance when the land was cultivated by the proprietors themselves and the rights of sub-tenants did not come into question. Again, it was not only in the joint villages that a distinction between two classes of occupants existed, and the local offices would commonly be filled by members of the oldest families. Rights over the waste could constitute but little difference as long as population was sparse and land plentiful. Finally, the two classes of villages were from various causes constantly passing into each other[3].

The Village and the State. The relation of the political unit to the state is implied in the double functions of the village officers, who were on the one hand the nominees and representatives of the rayats, and on the other functionaries of the king. The rights of the burghers never extended to the possession of the land in fee simple, but constituted merely a claim to permanent occupancy on condition of paying the royal portion. They were inalienable, and on the disappearance of the owners by death or inability to pay returned again into the hands

[1] *Vide* Baden-Powell, *op. cit.* pp. 51 sqq., and Campbell, *Modern India*, pp. 8, 9.

[2] Baden-Powell, *Ibid.* p. 71.

[3] *Ibid.* pp. 73—75.

of the community.   Nor again did the real ownership apper-
tain to the king.   In fact the conception of full and clear
ownership is a product of western thought.   In India the
theory of Dharma, in which so many different conceptions
lie confused and latent, contains also the native theory of
land-tenure.   The cultivators are the *vaisyas* of the Brahmanical Law.   They are the 'thighs' of the national body,
and the importance of their functions is often exalted in
the books.   The whole theory of Hindu society is expressed
in a verse of Manu : 'To carry arms for striking and throw-
'ing is prescribed for Kshatriyas as a means of subsistence;
'to trade, to rear cattle, and agriculture for the Vaisyas.'
Commerce and agriculture were the *duties* of the Vaisyas
class.   The Creator had ordained that they should contribute
the necessaries of life for the whole community.   Meanwhile
the Kshatriya was left free for the performance of his special
functions, to preserve intact the sacred institutions of caste
and to defend the people from foreign enemies.   This was
the sacred office which entitled the lord of the Kshatriyas to
his portion of the yearly tribute of the earth, and the Law
knows of no baser character than the king, who, exacting his
sixth part, yet fails to uphold and to protect.

    In what manner then were the remaining members of the *The Kshatri-yas.*
warrior caste maintained, since they were forbidden, except
under pressure of necessity, to engage in trade and agriculture ?   They were maintained out of the royal taxes, but in
different ways.   Some formed the immediate court and body-
guard of the king.   Great numbers were stationed in forts
throughout the country[1] and especially on the frontier.
These enjoyed regular salaries and allowances from the royal
chest.   But there were also two other sources of subsistence
for the Kshatriya.   The king was ruler and administrator as
well as warrior, and above the village Headmen, who were
his servants, maintained various grades of officials.   He is
directed[2] to appoint not only rulers of single villages, but also
rulers of twenty, one hundred, and a thousand respectively,

[1] Manu vii. 114, Hiuen-Thsang (Beal) i. pp. 82 and 87.
[2] Manu vii. 115—7.

forming a continuous gradation from the lowest to the highest. Each of these was a king in miniature, being at once revenue officer, magistrate, and governor. Each had his personal retainers and swordsmen, and to each was assigned a special source of maintenance, consisting of grants of land or per- centages of the revenue. 'The ruler of a hundred villages 'ought to have to supply his needs the revenue derived 'from one whole flourishing town, while the thousand-village- 'man has a large city, gold, grain, &c. appropriated to his 'use[1].' The officers, of whom the last and most important survived in Muhammadan times under the title of *karori*, together with their retainers, belonged mainly to the Kshat- riya caste. It has been thought that their position some- times approximated rather closely to that of the modern *zamindar*. This is probably untrue; but that the growth and exercise of their powers needed careful supervision is shown by the special provision of a body of spies, whose duty it was in the interests of the king and the rayats alike to keep the king well informed of all their proceedings[2]. A second safeguard was provided by the appointment of parallel grades of accountants and finance officers from the village *patwari* upwards, men in a stricter sense the king's officers[3]. These were probably either Brahmans or, as we should gather from the Greek accounts, men of special caste; at any rate they would not be Kshatriyas.

The third source from which the Kshatriyas derived their maintenance reveals a second division of the lands of the ancient Hindu kingdoms, presenting interesting analogies to certain phenomena of western constitutional history. What has been said above applies only to the King's Domain, or the *khálsa* land—to use a term of later date. This embraced the best cultivated territory, and especially the central region in the kingdom. The wilder parts, and in particular the

---

[1] *Vide* Manu vii. 119, and E. W. Hopkins, *Position of the Ruling Caste in Ancient India*, in *Journal of American Oriental Society*, Vol. v.: also Hiuen- Thsang (Beal) i. p. 88.

[2] Manu vii. 122—3, and the Greek authorities Arrian, Strabo, &c.

[3] Manu vii. 80—1.

border districts, were administered on a different system. They were held by Kshatriyas on tenure of military service. The relations which these *jagirdars*—as their successors were called in Muhammadan times—bore to the king corresponded even in certain details to the institutions of European feudalism[1]. The independent spirit which it fostered was the same. The meanest and poorest of the warrior caste deemed himself in a sense the equal of the king, and the power of this order was the chief check upon his aggrandisement. To a good king on the other hand their devotion, based on the sense of relationship and the far stronger obligation of caste, would manifest all the unswerving fidelity of the Hindu character. This faithfulness has been at all times eulogized even by those who have taken the lowest view of native morality[2], and even at the time of the Mutiny numbers of Englishmen were indebted to it for their lives. The desperate valour with which the Muhammadan invasion was resisted could not indeed overcome the evils of division, but it should serve to defend the Hindus in general—if defence were needed—from the charge of cowardice so often brought against them[3]. There is a Sanskrit verse which says, ' In this ' world, unstable as a wind-tossed wave, death for another's ' sake is a boon earned by good deeds in previous births.'

To complete this general description of the constitution of ancient Hindu society, it remains to mention the Brahmanical order and the facts of caste-division. The authority of the Brahmans, who were everywhere present and were maintained by royal grants[4] and freewill gifts from the

The Brahmans and Caste.

---

[1] *Vide* esp. Tod's *Annals of Rajasthan*, and in particular Vol. i. pp. 1—200, and for the differences, Lyall's *Asiatic Studies*, pp. 211 sqq.

[2] The Rev. Mr Terry for instance, who was Sir Thomas Roe's chaplain at the Mughal court in Jahangir's reign, while very severe on the native morality, yet enlarges on their faithfulness: *v.* Kerr's *Voyages*, ix. p. 402. Cf. Sleeman's *Rambles*, i. 309, 310.

[3] No reader of Tod's *Annals of Rajasthan* can overlook this characteristic of the Hindus under their native rulers: *v.* esp. i. pp. 193 sqq. Compare the words of the *Ain-i-Akbari*, ' Their soldiers know not what it is to fly in battle.'

[4] These existed in vast numbers in ancient times and under the Mahrattas. But in the confusion which attended the English conquest they have in great measure passed away.

people, was conceived to be in a special sense based upon divine legislation. They were, indeed, as the Buddhist king Aṣoka had inscribed on one of his rock edicts three centuries before Christ, the real gods of Brahmanism. But the exercise of this authority in affairs of state depended, as did the authority of the Church in mediaeval Europe, on the character and strength of the king. The victory would seem to have rested with the state. In the Sanskrit dramas the Brahman minister becomes the Vidūshaka, a kind of holy parasite, treated with outward courtesy but made ridiculous at every turn. Among the people, however, the authority of this caste, not seldom based on a real devotion to their office and caste duties, must have been practically without limit.

The system of the four castes never existed in more than name as a past ideal, except in Hindustan, and even here we must exclude Lower Bengal and the Indus region. The peninsula exhibited in Hindu times an even more primitive stage of society: there was, so far as we know, little trace of a warrior caste and sometimes not even a king, but only Brahman, cultivator, and low-caste. Further, even in Hindustan the Vaiṣya caste was everywhere much divided into smaller bodies, and one only in name, if so much. Mixed castes were innumerable. Not seldom the warrior sank and mingled with inferior classes[1], and in some parts the line between Kshatriyas and Vaiṣyas was very fluctuating. Even in native India personal genius sometimes served to elevate a low-caste or an outcast, and Hiuen-Thsang mentions more than one Ṣūdra king[2]. Vaishnavism had already begun to exercise its dissolving influence. But, speaking generally, the constitution of the native governments was down to the time of the Muhammadan irruption, in Hindustan at any rate, of the character we have described, distinguished from European feudalism by circumstances of time and place, but chiefly by the one great

[1] Provision is made for this case in the law books: v. Manu x. 83—95.

[2] Cf. the beautiful story of the Kshatriya soldier and the Ṣūdra king, Hitopadeṣa III. It is curious that Hiuen-Thsang (Beal) i. p. 82 sets down the Ṣūdra and not the Vaiṣya as the agricultural class: cf. Sir W. W. Hunter, *India*, p. 91.

characteristic that the divisions of society were based on race *To be done* and consecrated under the name of caste as a divine ordinance.

The amount of revenue exacted by the native princes, and *Amount of revenue exacted.* the law which they administered, deserve a brief mention. The text of Manu on the first of these subjects runs as follows :—' A fiftieth part of (the increments on) cattle and ' gold may be taken by the king, and the eighth, sixth, or ' twelfth part of the crops. He may also take the sixth part ' of trees, meat, honey, clarified butter, perfumes, herbs, sub-' stances used for flavouring food, flowers, roots, and fruits ; ' of leaves, pot-herbs, grass, objects made of cane, skins, of ' earthen vessels, and all articles made of stone. . . . Let the ' king make the common inhabitants of his realm who live by ' traffic pay annually some trifle, which is called a tax. ' Mechanics and artisans as well as Ṣudras, who subsist by ' manual labour, he may cause to work one day in each month. ' Let him not cut up his own root (by levying no taxes), nor ' the root of others by excessive greed; for by doing so he ' makes himself and them wretched[1].'

In time of war or distress the king might exact a larger proportion, even one-fourth, of the crops. But so firmly was the sixth held to be his proper share that he is commonly intitled *shadbhāgin,* ' one whose share is one-sixth.' Whether he took one-fourth or one-sixth it was believed if he failed ' to protect the people ' in the proper degree he incurred in the same proportion the guilt of their sins. ' That monarch ' whose subjects are carried off by robbers from his kingdom, ' while they loudly call for help, and he and his servants are ' looking on, is a dead and not a living king[2].'

So much for the legal claim. The proportion actually exacted we are not in a position to estimate with certainty. But the strength of native custom in these matters leads us to believe that the fact corresponded to the demands of the law ; especially when we remember that in the form of dues and cesses on various occasions, such as marriage, coming of

---

[1] Manu VII. 130 sqq. trans. Bühler.
[2] Manu VII. 143.

age, betrothal of a daughter, and the like, further sums could
be demanded, and that in case of disaster part of the loss
could be recovered from the subjects. The Chinese Buddhist
pilgrim, Fa-Hian, wrote early in the fifth century:—'The
'people are very well off without poll-tax or official restric-
'tions. Only those who till the royal lands return a portion
'of the profit of the land[1]:' and again :—'The people are rich
'and prosperous[2].' Hiuen-Thsang writes two centuries later
to the same effect, and definitely states the royal revenue at
one-sixth of the produce[3]. In short every indication tends to
prove that in pre-Muhammadan times India, with its small
kingdoms, was neither strong nor united, but happy. Under
the Muhammadan and even under the English he may well
look back with regret upon the ancient paternal government
of his Kshatriya king, when war was his only enemy. Even
at the present day and in Bengal the native zamindar rarely
attempts to push his advantage to the utmost, and is for the
most part content with his traditional dues centuries old.
'Perhaps the ryot might fare worse than under his King Log
sort of rule[4].' Before the Musalman came, when land was
plentiful and cultivators in demand, it was impossible to
oppress them beyond a certain point, predial servitude being
practically unknown and flight to a more favoured village
always open. 'If they desire to go, they go; if they like to
'stop, they stop' writes Fa-Hian[5]. The proprietary holders,
by whom I mean the governing families in the villages, were
less willing to emigrate and could be more highly taxed than
others, bound by slighter ties to the land. But this could
not proceed beyond a certain point, and they were often
entitled to dues from inferior holders, whereby partly to
recoup the extra burden.

Law. The subject of Law is one of the most difficult parts of
Indian antiquities. There have been handed down to us a
number of ancient metrical treatises, called Dharmaśāstras,

---

[1] Beal, *Buddhist Records of the Western World*, p. xxxvii.
[2] *Ibid.* p. lvi.   [3] *Ibid.* p. 87.
[4] Campbell, *Land Tenure in India*, p. 183.
[5] Beal, *op. cit.* p. xxxvii.

containing precepts on law, morality, and religion. The two most important of these, ascribed to Manu and Yājñavalkya, treat the subject of law in considerable detail, and so far provide ample material for a discussion of the subject. But it has now been established that these books should be compared, not with modern codes, but with such semi-religious compilations as the book of Leviticus, concerning which it is uncertain how far they were ever followed in practice. They are books of the schools[1]. Not only so, but they are based on older compilations attached to special Vedic schools, and contain the customs and theories of sections, not of the whole of the Brahmanical body. This last consideration is however of less moment in consequence of the universal acceptance in the schools which the treatises had won in the latest Hindu period. They did not demand implicit obedience in every particular—though the authority of the parts grew with that of the whole—but exhibited the general principles and theory of administration, to be modified indefinitely by local circumstance and usage. In short, they held a position similar in kind to that of the law of Islam, depending in theory upon revelation and in fact upon the influence of the learned class that supplied or advised the king's officers.

The administration of the law would then follow such lines as these. Of written law in our sense there was little : a few royal decrees, grants of monopolies, and minor regulations of various kinds[2]. These were literally binding. On the other hand, every village authority, every district official, superior or inferior, was empowered to act as judge in cases connected with his duties, to settle disputes, exact revenue, and punish offenders. Herein they would chiefly follow the customary law, modified by the principles of the Dharmaśāstras as interpreted by Brahman assessors. But various classes of cases were reserved for the jurisdiction of higher officials and of the king himself[3], who, like the Musalman

---

[1] Manu is sometimes held to have been a semi-popular work. The same could not be said of Nārada, Brhaspati &c., which are strictly scientific.

[2] Such as appear in the inscriptions.

[3] *Vide* Manu vii. 116—7.

emperors, always passed a portion of his day in trying cases[1]. Before him would come all the most important criminal cases, and here the law of the schools, though the king's will could always set it aside, would have a much higher importance than elsewhere. The special provisions of the sacred texts would in this sphere be based on practice and literally followed. Yet, since the king and his officers were regarded as embodiments of the law, their judgments admitted of no appeal. Still in the region of criminal law we may assign a considerable degree of authority to the law of the books[2].

Obviously such a system, lax, indefinite, and depending largely on unwritten custom, was inconsistent with the existence of widely extended and highly centralised empires. Accordingly, as was said, we have evidence to prove that, except during very brief periods, India was divided into small kingdoms under independent rulers, and we hear only very rarely of more extensive governments. Not only is this truth supported by the indications in the native literature, and by the Muhammadan accounts of the conquest, but we have the evidence of independent witnesses in the reports of the Chinese travellers, especially of Hiuen-Thsang, a Buddhist pilgrim, who visited India in the 7th century and has given us accounts of as many as seventy kingdoms which he visited there. He tells us of kingdoms of now 200 miles, now 400, now 1000 in circuit, each with its own king, government, and laws. Now and again he speaks of a country as subject to one of its neighbours, and he mentions an occasion when eighteen kings rowed the barge of the king of Kanauj on the Ganges. But from his narrative and from other sources we gather that this subjection was commonly limited to admission of feudal superiority, liability to pay tribute, and service in war. Sometimes the king was deposed; but on the whole interference with internal administration was extremely rare. It was introduced by the Muhammadan rulers and not by the earliest even of these.

Résumé.   Enough has now been said to convey a general conception

---

[1] The Dramas here support the testimony of the law-books.

[2] Cf. esp. Burnell's Introduction to his Translation of Manu, p. xxxiv.

of the constitution of society in pre-Muhammadan India. The account is true only in outline, and would be falsified by the addition of details, which varied indefinitely in the different provinces. We have seen that of law, in our sense of the term, there was but little, its place being supplied on the one hand by custom, and on the other by the authority of heads of castes, village magistrates, and royal officers. The law-books of the Brahmans are rather expressions of the theories and prepossessions of their authors, than digests of enact-ments really carried into practice, and it is even uncertain to what proportion of the people they were really designed to apply. They can never have been more than morally binding on the rulers, and the offences which they denounce are con-ceived of rather in the light of sins than of crimes. It is only under the English that they have been actually employed in practice.

In enquiring therefore how far the law of the Hindus and *How far* of the Muhammadans exercised mutual influence, we are not *mutual in-* asking—at any rate primarily—what traces of Hindu theories *fluence can* are to be found in the Muhammadan books or vice versâ. *be traced.* Such an inquiry would be in the main both irrelevant and fruitless. Both systems having been matured long before they came into contact, the commentaries, monographs, and digests, which we owe to the industry of the eight centuries from the tenth to the eighteenth, are mainly the work of scholars, not of jurists, and belong more to exegetic theology than to law proper. We must look at the subject from the point of view of history. We must ask what changes in native society can be shown to be effects of the Musalman rule, and in particular how the rights of landowners and tenants, the basis of that society, were affected: how far the Muhammadan theories were adapted to a polity for which they were not framed: to what extent the administration of justice changed hands: and finally, so far as scattered notices allow, what was the nature of the law actually followed, and how much of it is to be traced to Hindu and how much to Musalman sources.

Three periods are to be traced in the dominion of the *Three periods of Musalman rule.* Musalmans in India. During the first of these, which commences with the invasions of Mahmud of Ghazni, in the eleventh century, and extends to the beginning of the thirteenth, a considerable part of Hindustan was conquered and became a tributary dependency of dynasties ruling at Ghazni and Ghor beyond the frontier. The second period ends with the Mughal conquest, completed under Babar about the year 1530. During the two first centuries of this period a succession of Musalman dynasties governing from Delhi brought practically the whole of the peninsula, with the exception of Orissa, under their dominion. But during the last two centuries of this period there was a complete dissolution of the empire of Delhi, due in the first place to the mismanagement of Muhammad Tughlak (1325–1351) and to the devastating invasion of Tamerlane (1398). Bengal was severed (1340) for two centuries from the rest of Hindustan, and all India south of the Vindhya remained up to the time of Akbar entirely independent and divided between a number of Hindu and Muhammadan kingdoms. The third period, ending for our purpose about the middle of the eighteenth century, saw the empire first of all consolidated and enlarged to nearly its former dimensions under Babar, Humayun, and Akbar, culminating for a moment under Aurangzib, and commencing during the latter part of this reign, a process of dissolution which was continually accelerated under the emperors who succeeded.

Characteristics of Government during the three periods. These three periods were characterised on the whole by three different methods of treating the people and the land. During the first period, though tribute was exacted, there was scarcely any interference with the native governments. When Mahmud of Ghazni conquered Guzarat in 1024 A.D., the country was not annexed, but, the rájá refusing to submit, another member of the same family was set on the throne, an example of a policy which was very generally pursued. But when Hindustan became an independent Muhammadan kingdom, and with a Muhammadan court at Delhi members of the faith began to settle in the country, the internal management of the provinces came to be taken under the direct control of the imperial power; tribute ceased, and in its place the whole revenue accrued to the treasury, while the rájá either disappeared or sank into the status of an official. This process, though constantly interrupted, must have been continually advancing. Hence in the third period, when Akbar came to fix his settlement, Hindustan could be treated as a single whole, and the tributary prince and the hereditary zamindar were scarcely considered.

But, while these three periods may be in this way distin- *Material* guished, it must not be imagined that the materials at our $\frac{for the}{enquiry.}$ disposal enable us to consider them separately in detail. On such questions as these we are treating the material of history is exceedingly scanty, and all that we are permitted to do is to take the gross amount of change effected during the Muhammadan rule, to analyse it, and to construct, so far as possible, the development of the several components. The heads under which we shall proceed to treat the subject will be three in number, namely Land System and Revenue, Management of Land Revenue, Administration, and Government, and in the third place Law.

Land System and Revenue.

According to the Muhammadan law, conquered or ceded *Muham-* territory may be either confiscated or left in the hands of its *madan* original owner. In the latter case it is subject to a land tax, *Land* *charág*, and this tax may be imposed in either of two ways. *Tenure.* It may take the form of a fixed payment exacted on a whole area or on each unit of land after measurement: or it may consist of a demand for a proportion of the produce, which need never fall below, and must never exceed, a moiety. In the former case it is termed the '*muwazzaf*' and in the latter the '*mokásamah*' charág[1]. These differences imply also a distinction of right, it being held that under the 'mokásamah'

---

[1] On these cesses, cf. Kremer, *Culturgeschichte* &c., I. 277—8, 437—8, and *Ayeen Akbery*, I. p. 280.

form of the tax the ownership of the land rests with the state, while under the 'muwazzaf' it rests with the cultivator.

It will be seen that the Muhammadan theory did not differ widely from that of the Hindus themselves. The mokâsamah charâg bore much the closer resemblance to the native system; but the tenure of those rayats whom we have described as permanent occupiers was in so far analogous to the muwazzaf charâg that a fine was inflicted for neglect to cultivate their land[1].

Changes introduced into the Hindu system. It was no doubt due in part to this general resemblance that the native system was little affected by the conquest. But the chief cause of this is rather to be found in the comparative fewness of the invaders, the tardy completion of the conquest, and the necessity of employing native officers in this department of government. Unable to rid itself of the native officials, the state could scarcely effect a sweeping change of method, and remained content so long as its portion of the produce came punctually in. Up to the time of Akbar no great change—if we neglect the temporary provisions of Ala-ud-din (1295–1316)—had been imported into the traditional system. In one direction indeed -there had been momentous changes, namely in the proportion of the harvest exacted by the Government. The sixth permitted by the Hindu law had been constantly enhanced. The moiety demanded by the law of Islam was steadily kept in sight, and Ala-ud-din attempted to exact it in full[2]; and though this attempt came to an end at his death, yet some considerable advance towards that goal had undoubtedly taken place.

The first revolution in land tenure, and so far as concerns Muhammadan times also the last, was enacted by Akbar, the greatest of the emperors, whose settlement has formed the basis of all its successors. Its effect was to substitute a fixed demand in place of a proportion of the produce. The land under cultivation was divided into equal parts called '*bigas*,' measuring somewhat more than half an acre. The average

---

[1] Phillips, *Tagore Law Lectures for* 1875, pp. 45—48. Manu VIII. 243.

[2] *Vide* Phillips, *ibid.* p. 54.

produce of a *biga* was determined, and the maximum demand was fixed at one-third, payable in specie, according to an average of prices estimated over nineteen preceding years. The settlement was at first during its experimental stage annual, but afterwards it was fixed by periods of ten years[1]. The object of the reform being to relieve the depression of the rayats, its application as a whole and in several of its parts was optional. Thus every rayat who was dissatisfied with the demand might 'insist on an actual measurement 'and division of the crop,' or, if the established rate of prices seemed too high, was at liberty to pay his tax in kind. He was at the same time relieved, as we are informed, from a number of vexatious dues and cesses[2].

The whole scheme was carried out in great detail. Every provision was made for lands of different natural value, for differences of irrigation, and similar conditions. The surviving records in the Ain-i-Akbari (Ayeen Akbery) and elsewhere have enabled Mr Thomas to calculate with some exactitude the amount of revenue derived by Akbar and his successors from the land. The land-revenue usually constituted somewhat less than one-half of the total income of the state. In Akbar's day it averaged about seventeen millions sterling. In the year 1628, under Jahangir the full amount was seventeen and a half millions. Thenceforward it steadily increased until under Aurangzib it attained its maximum of nearly thirty-nine millions sterling[3], an increase due partly to an enhanced assessment and partly to an enlargement of the empire. From a much wider area of cultivated land the British Government now derives slightly over seventeen millions. We must however not fail to mention that these figures, which are taken from the revised statement in the *Gazetteer of India* (art. 'India,' vol. VI 298-9), have been questioned by General Cunningham, who not only combats certain details, but also denies that the demand can ever

---

[1] On the above *v. Ayeen Akbery* (Gladwin 1800), I. p. 292—4.

[2] Including the *jizya* or poll-tax on unbelievers. A list of remitted taxes is given in the *Ayeen Akbery* (Gladwin 1800), I. 288.

[3] In the year 1697.

have been realised in full.   Mr Thomas, however, stands by
his original opinion[1].

The new assessment was not everywhere introduced at
once, and in the Deccan it was not Akbar's but Malik Ambar's
settlement that prevailed.   This is however of less importance, since when Malik Ambar, minister at the court of
Ahmadnagar, introduced his system in the years 1610–1614,
he followed the earlier scheme in all its main outlines with
slight variation[2].

Aim and effects of Akbar's settlement.   Akbar's settlement was in every way a great reform.   It
aimed at introducing regularity and order into what had
previously been a chaos.   It formed a part of Akbar's great
scheme for the unification of India.   This is seen not only in
the application of the settlement to the whole empire, but
also in the abolition of the hated poll-tax, the mark of subjection and of severance between the conquerors and the
conquered.   Todar Mall, who was employed by the emperor
to carry out the settlement and whose name it often bears,
was himself a Hindu rājā.   But the settlement was a great
measure of philanthropy as well as of administration, re-
voking numberless usurpations and abuses[3] and substituting
the precision of law for the pleasure of officials.   Many of its
provisions remain in operation, and its principle of dealing
with the individual cultivator[4] is still followed in the territories of Bombay and Madras.

The above is practically the sum of the changes introduced into the Hindu land system by the direct enactments
of the Musalman rulers.   Whether it involved any such
transfer of rights as is implied in the ' muwazzaf charâg ' is a
matter for dispute[5] and of only theoretical importance.

---

[1] Originally put forward in his *Revenues of the Mughal Emperors* (1871),
and based chiefly on the Ain-i-Akbari and the accounts of European travellers.

[2] *Vide* Grant-Duff, *History of the Mahrattas* (Bombay Ed.), I. 70—1, and
Elphinstone (Ed. 3), p. 486.

[3] Including a great number of tolls at city gates, fords, &c.

[4] 'Let him (the Amilguzzar) transact his business with each husbandman
separately,' *Ayeen Akbery*, I. 305.

[5] Phillips, *op. cit.* pp. 48 sq.

Akbar's predecessors had found it from the nature of the case impossible to do anything but accept the system which they found, or had only so far modified it as to exact a much enhanced revenue. His successors were content to accept the fruits of his labours, and, if nothing else, the speedy decline of the empire must have rendered it impossible to give heed to constructive legislation. When the English arrived, the rayat was paying to the state on the average about three-fifths of the produce of his land, retaining only two-fifths to repay his expenses and unremitting labours. His tenure, except in cases where he had sunk to the position of tenant-at-will under his zamindar, remained what it had always been and what the personal character of Hindu and Muhammadan law encouraged, a right to permanent occupancy on condition of paying the fixed or customary dues of the state.

Management of Land Revenue, Administration and Government.

We have seen in what precedes that in Hindu times the land was held on tenures of two different kinds, the royal domain in the centre paying revenue to the king, and the border or hill territory held by the nobles on condition of military service. Now what would be the first effect of the Muhammadan conquest? The cultivators would only in rare cases take part in the struggle[1]. The fighting would be done by the king and the Kshatriyas, and from the sanguinary character of the conflict we may infer that a considerable extent of territory must have lost its owners. This would not be to so great an extent the case with the kingdoms which at once submitted to the payment of tribute. The native governments seldom submitted without a struggle. Yet as it was not at first the policy of the

First effects of the Conquest.

---

[1] Cf. what the Greek authorities recount on the subject.

invaders to interfere with internal affairs, they for the most part maintained the monarchical constitution of the native states, and when they deposed one king commonly replaced him with a more submissive member of his family. Hence the first effect of the conquest would be to shatter the power and numbers of the native nobles and to deprive them of their raison d'être. The lands which became vacant would fall to the disposal of the king, and be added to the revenue-paying domain. Thus the first effect of the conquest was on the one hand to weaken the nobles, and on the other to strengthen the internal authority of the king and provide him with means of paying his tribute to the conqueror.

Later changes. But as the power of the Musalmans consolidated, and in place of a fixed tribute they began to claim the whole revenue of the land as their due, the position both of the Kshatriyas and of the king was completely overturned. The Musalman government could not recognize the feudal tenure of the nobles, and their estates as well as the royal domain incurred the obligation of paying the land tax. Thus the Kshatriyas lapsed, and except in those parts of India which were never permanently subdued, as for instance in Raj-putana, no trace of their position survives. Not that their estates at once passed from their hands; but instead of enjoying their income in full they retained only a certain portion as the agency through which the remainder was transmitted to the state. Thus arose an intermediate tenure between the government and the actual cultivator. The rājā shared the fate of the Kshatriyas. Either he was removed or he subsisted as a pensioner of the state or an agent for transmitting its revenue.

The jagir. But while the old feudal relations of the nobles to their local rājās thus passed away, a new system of feuds arose as the direct creation of the Musalman governments. It was the practice of the Muhammadan government, never strong enough itself to maintain the peace through its vast empire, to allot grants of land revenue-free to its servants. These *jagir* grants, as they were called, were assigned for various objects. Some were religious; others were marks of favour shown to individuals. But the vast majority of them had a distinct place in the machinery of government. They were granted for the most part to Muhammadan soldiers, whose business it was on the one hand to provide for the police regulations of their district, on the other hand to keep in check the local rājās or inferior magnates, and curb their encroachments. For the latter purpose they were provided with bodies of retainers, and they acted the part of garrisons throughout the country. So important was this safeguard of the Muhammadan rule that it is calculated that no less than two-fifths of the whole area of the empire was held on this tenure[1]. Without it India could never have been permanently retained by the Muhammadans. Though the holders must have been for the most part Musalmans, yet many native rājās and nobles would undertake these duties and thus maintain a semblance of their original power. In point of right the main difference between the Hindu and Muhammadan systems was that in the former the tenure was hereditary, while in the latter the jagir reverted to the state on the death of the holder[2]. Yet in fact the hereditary principle commonly prevailed, especially when the central government was weak, and the granting of the new *sanad* to the incoming heir became a matter of form, costing only a present to the governor[3]. But such outward resemblances as subsisted between the two systems cannot conceal the complete contrast in intention. Under his local rājā the Hindu noble held his feud as a part of the divine constitution of society, and the king was only the somewhat more powerful head of his tribe and caste. But the jagirdar of Muhammadan times was the representative of a distant and mighty emperor, removable at pleasure and settled amid an alien population which it was his business to overawe. Nevertheless a considerable number of Hindus must always have been recognized as jagirdars simply because it was impossible to get rid of them, and any pindhari chief who made

---

[1] Phillips, p. 81.
[2] *Fifth Report*, p. 86.
[3] Cf. Baden-Powell, *op. cit.* p. 632.

himself sufficiently troublesome might be reconciled to the government on similar terms. The grand schemes of the 'King of the Mountains' in About's tale are often crowned with success in the East.

The zamindari. So much for the Musalman system of the *jagirdari*, under which many of the Hindu ruling caste must have survived. Coming to the *zamindari*, wherein most relics of the ancient *raj* remain, we have to make the oft-repeated observation that the word covers two different classes of persons, the village *zamindars* of the North-West and the *zamindars* of the great estates of Lower Bengal. In the North-West there is commonly no class possessing rights on the land between the state and the joint-village owners or village zamindars, who treat directly with it. Their status will come under consideration below. Here we have only to point out the connection between the history of the North-West and the absence of a landlord class. It is here that Muhammadanism has most thoroughly done its work. Here was the scene of the historic battles. Here the Musalmans settled in the largest numbers, and here their power had been longest established. Consequently it was here that the native aristocracy most completely disappeared. Where the villages are strong the zamindars are weak or non-existent. Where the zamindars are strong, the village organisation is relaxed, and the power of the Musalman government has never been at its height.

The beginnings of the zamindari, as we found it in Bengal, are to be traced in Hindu times. It has been observed that the *chaudari* 'the lord of a thousand villages' (the *karori* of the Muhammadans, and the *crory* of the English) was in some measure the predecessor of the zamindar. The chief difference between the two lies in the fact that the zamindar had, while his predecessor had not, the right to dispose of the waste. It is thought that the zamindari was a very early product of the conquest. The Hindu rājās, finding that their standing was becoming more and more precarious, proceeded to sell their rights over the waste to their *chaudaris*, who thus attained at once to the full powers of the zamindari. Be that as it may, the zamindars appear early in the history of the Muhammadan empire, and it is clear that the *chaudari* is one of the officials from whom they arose.

More commonly, however, it was the rājā himself who became zamindar, and it was to such hereditary chiefs that the term seems originally to have been applied[1]. When he could no longer maintain his independence, he became a servant of the state. In quiet times he would accept the necessity of his position and retain only the allowances which were his due. But his ancient claims were long remembered, and the slightest symptom of weakness on the part of his master was a signal for their resumption.

But while in the main it is from the rājās and the chaudaris that the zamindars are derived, it was by no means only from these. Robber chiefs were often permitted to exercise the functions of the zamindari in districts which they had terrorized. Revenue officials constantly so far encroached as to establish themselves on this firm footing. And when in the later times of the empire the system of farming the revenue came into fashion, this also was a means of increasing the numbers of this class. When the English arrived, almost the whole of Lower Bengal and Bahar was held by zamindars. In Oudh the *taluqdars* exercised much the same rights. In the south they scarcely existed, though they do appear in the polygars of Madras and in districts of the Central Provinces[2]. In the North-West as we have seen they did not occur.

The position of the zamindar and taluqdar represents the point at which the Hindu and Muhammadan systems came into collision. Every Hindu office or function tends to become hereditary[3]. Election is soon reduced to a mere form, which often survives long after the reality has vanished. Muhammadanism on the other hand has in consequence of its doctrine of equality always favoured imperialism and

---

[1] Elphinstone, (Ed. 3), p. 422.
[2] *Vide* Baden-Powell, p. 441.
[3] *Vide* Patton's *Asiatic Monarchies, passim.*

resisted the growth of a hereditary aristocracy. In India the official ranks below the zamindar were almost entirely Hindu, those above for the most part Musalman, and it is at the status of the zamindar and taluqdar that the two systems met.   When the empire consolidated and fixed tribute gave way to a demand for the revenue in full, the rājā, reduced to an official, was allowed for his remuneration a fixed proportion of the revenue along with remission of taxation on such land as he himself cultivated.   For the rest most of his old rights remained, both judicial and administrative, and he retained so much sense of his original position that he felt that the succession should descend to his son, and that he was justified in extending his powers in every way.   The Muhammadan government, on the other hand, while willing to accept this inheritance of officers in practice, yet refused to admit its theoretic validity, and insisted upon the incomer's applying for instalment by the state.   The duties were, it is true, for the most part entered upon before the customary presents were sent and the *sanad* claimed and granted; but until the last the state continued to uphold the theory that the tenure of office issued from itself and was revocable at pleasure.   Hence the official rights and functions were originally, at any rate, inalienable.   It sometimes happened however that, when the zamindar objected to the assessment in any particular year, he was permitted to dispose of his rights to some one more compliant, and himself retire in possession of certain allowances.   But even here the sanction of the state was theoretically necessary; though it seems so frequently to have been neglected that this proceeding gave rise in later times to the regular alienation of the zamindari.   The Musalman government was not generally anxious to rid itself of this status, and consequently failed to make use of these opportunities.   But in earlier times whenever the rājā refused to become a revenue official or was not accepted as such, he would be at once dismissed with or without some form of pension, while the chaudari would treat with the government and become in time zamindar.

In this manner the zamindar is seen encroaching on the *Farming of the Revenue.* powers of the central government. He has acquired, or at least maintained, the rights of permanency and alienation. He has full power to dispose of the waste. But he encroached also in other ways. At various times and especially towards the close of the Mughal rule the weakness of the state gave rise to a system of farming the revenue. The contractor was entitled *amil*, and he was supported by a body of troops and other means of enforcing his demand. Now it is clear that such a person was a formidable rival of the zamindars. No doubt he often succeeded in making their position intolerable, driving them out, and usurping their place; so that, as was observed above, this was one of the classes from which zamindars arose. But in general the system strengthened the hands of the zamindars; for it was with them that the contract was commonly made. In such cases the state practically gave up all control over the collection of the revenue, and the exactions of the zamindar ceased to bear any relation to the receipts of the treasury. The rayat was completely at his mercy, and his position must have been grievously affected.

This brings us to the encroachments of the zamindars on *Encroachment on the rights of inferiors.* the rights of those beneath them. When the English arrived matters had reached in Bengal such a pass that it was difficult to distinguish the zamindar from the English landlord[1]. The rayats, originally permanent occupants, had sunk very commonly into the condition of tenants-at-will, and their only protection was that law of custom which neither zamindar nor rayat could help respecting. This had come to pass in various ways. In the first place the right to dispose of the waste had been a source of immense profit. Whereas under the ancient rājās cultivation had in practice been open to all on condition of paying the royal dues, the zamindars accorded permission to till the waste only on terms of tenancy-at-will. Again, they had always been allowed certain stretches of land rent free—the so-called *nankar* land—in part payment of their services; and these it

---

[1] *Vide* Baden-Powell, *op. cit.* p. 112.

was easy to make permanently their own. Thirdly, they consistently employed the opportunities of their position to subvert the rights of the rayats of even longest standing. In times of lax supervision it was easy so to adjust the burden of taxation as to render the position of the permanent occupier unbearable, to oust him completely, or to compel him to become a tenant[1]. In short, they left untried none of those artifices which the history of landownership exhibits in all parts of the world. They seized every opportunity of appropriating the powers of the headmen, whom in the end they converted from hereditary village officers into nominees and subordinates of their own; and as for the powers of the village and district accountants, who in times of order were the chief check upon their aggrandisement, they had, when the English came, either rendered them obsolete or made them serviceable to their own purposes[2]. In this way they greatly weakened the village organisation and in Bengal practically destroyed it. Dues and cesses they levied on every possible pretext, on the occasion of a marriage, a death, a festival, a present to the king, a misfortune, in short, on every opportunity that ingenuity could devise. Thus it sometimes came to pass that, when the state demand was one-half or one-third, they left the rayat with no more than one-tenth of the produce of the land, and to take only two-fifths or three-fifths was thought to display liberality.

Checks upon the zamindars. The Musalman government at various times made strenuous efforts to curb the power of the zamindars. Quite early in the history of the institution Ala-ud-din undertook their repression[3], and in Akbar's assessment they are mentioned only as needing restraint[4]. The rayat was encouraged

---

[1] *Vide* Baden-Powell, p. 112.

[2] *Ibid.* p. 112. Fifth Report, p. 17.

[3] Ferishta (Briggs), I. 347. 'He (Alla-ud-deen) appointed officers to superintend the revenue collectors, whose office it was to take care that the zemindars should demand no more from the cultivators than the estimate which the zemindars themselves had made.'

[4] They are mentioned in the Ayeen Akbery, I. 299, as needing repression. 'Whenever a zemindar, or a collector of the royal or jagir lands, is disobedient, he (the Foujdar) shall endeavour to bring him back to his duty by

to pay direct or through his headman to the officers of the treasury, and the additional exactions of the zamindars were swept away. But this only restrained them for a time, and during the latest period of the Musalman rule they were more flourishing than ever. The permanent means of control were represented by certain officials named respectively *amils* and *qanungos*, and their subordinates. The former, mentioned above as revenue-farmers, were originally charged with military and legal powers, commanding local detachments and maintained by jagir land. Like all other state officials they had a share in the administration of justice. The *qanungos* were accountants attached to districts (*parganas*), and corresponded to the village accountants (*patwaris*), who were their subordinates. We have had occasion to mention that both these offices were a survival from pre-Muhammadan times, and that where the zamindari was strong their authority was only nominal. In quiet times they were in direct connection with the state and formed a complete network of supervision throughout the land.

The zamindar attained his greatest development in Bengal. In Hindustan, the centre of the empire, the institution was never either common or strong. In the south, where it had once assumed considerable proportions, the Marhatta government, intolerant of middlemen, swept it away. The taluqdar, who like the zamindar in part represents the old Hindu rājā[1], arose in Bengal, the Central Provinces, and in Oudh. In Bengal he was sometimes a creation and dependant of the zamindar, sometimes independent or even superior. Thus, when Jaffir Khan in the time of Aurangzib attempted to abolish the former, the functions of the office fell to a great extent into the hands of the taluqdars. As to the difference between the two, it is held that the taluqdar did not require a *sanad* for the transmission of his rights, that his tenure was designedly more

The Taluqdar.

fair words: and if they fail........ If a number confederate together, let him fix his quarters near to their abode, and possess himself of their men and property by degrees, *without hazarding a general engagement.'*

[1] *Vide* Baden-Powell, *op. cit.* pp. 146, 385.

4—2

vague, his proprietorship more complete, and his lawful
emoluments of less amount, than in the case of the zamindar[1]. In Oudh the tenure was distinguished by the circumstance that the villages, being of the 'joint' or stronger
type, had retained their internal constitution unimpaired
and resisted interference and consequent decay.

*The
Villages.*   In tracing how it had fared with the ancient ruling caste
during the Musalman rule, we have had occasion to show
how the changes reacted upon the village in those parts
where the zamindari was in full swing. But little remains to
be added concerning the modifications which this political
unit underwent elsewhere. In the south, not only the de-
vastations, but also the deliberate policy of the Marhattas,
contributed to maintain the ancient character of the villages and to connect them directly with the Government;
whence its primitive type is nowhere to be seen in greater
purity than in this region. One change only has to be
noticed. In certain parts, and especially in what is now the
Central Provinces, the headman became to his village what
the zamindars were to their vast estates, not the revenue-
payer, but the landlord. The rayats sank, as under the
zamindars, to the status of tenants-at-will. This change is
held to have taken place chiefly during the later days of the
Marhatta rule, when, like the Musalmans, it had recourse to
the system of revenue-farming. But as it was the individual
villages which they commonly located and the headman
generally accepted the contract, it is chiefly from this class
that the modern village landlord, '*patel*' or '*carnam*,' is
derived. The contrary case of the contractor ousting the
headman must however have been frequent. In either case we
have a parallel to the development in Bengal, showing clearly
what is the inevitable issue of revenue-farming in India.

In the North-West Provinces and the Panjab the joint
villages have survived, and nearly the only zamindars are
those who most correctly bear the name[2], namely proprietary

---

[1] *Vide* Baden-Powell, *op. cit.* p. 385.

[2] Boulnois and Rattigan, *Customary Law in the Panjab.*

village occupiers of that class which was mentioned at the beginning of this chapter. But while it is allowable to speak of a revival, it is also true that the 'joint' village is to some extent also a new creation. The village zamindars are to a greater extent landlords, and have less to do with the actual tillage of the fields than in primitive times when as an agricultural people they divided a conquered territory among their families. Shadowy rights over the waste have given place to substantial incomes from tenants who till it. Sometimes what was once a common heritage has been allotted into shares, and in one group of cases the recollection of these shares has passed away. Again, the 'joint' village seems in many cases to have supplanted the more ancient type when great estates have been divided by inheritance, first of all into villages and then again into smaller shares. The land has often been assigned by the state in grants one upon the top of another, and each assignment has produced a new owner and converted the old into a tenant[1]. Thus in the case of these villages as of others the effect of the Musalman rule has been to multiply grades of tenure and keep the owner further from the land—a process hindered inside the village only by the equally persistent amalgamation of sub-tenures and above it by the direct communication between the local owners and the treasury.

We have now mentioned all the chief classes interested in *The Ranks above the Zamindar.* the land revenue, from the zamindar down to the actual cultivator of the soil. All above the last had so much in common that they were supported by jagirs, maintenance land, and percentages on the assessment. The amount of these percentages varied: the share of the zamindar would be about five per cent.[2]: that of the qanungo two and a half per cent.: and that of the patwari one per cent. Their rights were, according to the Muhammadan theory, revocable at pleasure; but in fact the Hindu hereditary principle almost

---

[1] *Vide* Baden-Powell, *op. cit.* pp. 352 sqq., 370, 374.

[2] Three-fiftieths acc. to the Fifth Report, p. 16. Baden-Powell and others state it at a tenth (*Land Systems, &c.* p. 112).

entirely prevailed[1], and investiture even in the case of the zamindar, where it was required, was nothing more than a formula.

In the ranks above the Muhammadan principle predominated. Transmission of the higher offices was so far from being the rule that it may be regarded as a symbol of independence. The chief provincial officer of state was the *sipah-sillar* or *subahdar*, the Musalman equivalent of our viceroy[2]. Akbar divided the empire into fifteen provinces or *subahs*, Allahabad, Agra, Oudh, Ajmir, Ahmadabad, Bahar, Bengal, Delhi, Kabul, Lahore, Multan, Malwa, Berar, Khandesh, and Ahmadnagar[3]. Each of these provinces was ruled by a subahdar, who represented the emperor in all his functions, as general, governor, and judge. Subdivisions, called *circars*, which in Akbar's time numbered nineteen in Bengal, and which were later superseded by *chuklas*, were under the military superintendence of *foujdars*[4], the administrative headship of *karoris*[5], and the revenue management of *amils*[6]. The *mir-i-adl* and the *kazi* shared the administration of justice, the latter stating the law and trying the case, the former passing sentence and ordering punishment[7].

Above the viceroy came the great officers and departments of state, all of purely Musalman origin, and differing widely from such Hindu institutions as most closely correspond to them. Thus the nearest parallel to the vizir is the Brahman minister or family priest[8], whose influence at the best of times was of an informal and religious character. Again, the rājā was most intimately acquainted with the interests of revenue and justice, while the army was placed

---

[1] The *qanungos* were generally Brahmans and their office was hereditary; *vide* Fifth Report, p. 633.

[2] *Vide* Ayeen Akbery, I. pp. 294 sqq.

[3] *Ibid.* II. 1 sqq.

[4] *Ibid.* I. 298—9.

[5] Who became hereditary : *vide* Phillips, p. 87.

[6] Ayeen Akbery, I. 303—9.

[7] *Ibid.* I. p. 300.

[8] The Rāmāyana supplies a good instance of a Brahman minister in the famous Vaṣishṭa.

under a commander-in-chief. But the great Musalman emperors had but little concern with the revenue department and brooked no commander-in-chief besides themselves. Even Akbar carried out his reforms through the agency of a Hindu rājā, Todar Mall. Lastly, there was no Musalman institution corresponding to the native council of seven advisers of the king.

If we now take a wide view of the changes which the con- *Summary.* stitution of native society sustained under the Musalman rule, we shall be at once struck by a certain incongruity between the agents and the effects. The ancient order of Hindu society, with its nobles, its Levites, its agricultural and semi-servile castes, was of very simple structure. No less simple is that order which Muhammadanism everywhere encourages, consisting on the one hand of an emperor with practically limitless powers, and on the other of a people saved from complete helplessness only by the influence of the religious order: the growth of aristocracy and of a strong middle class is inevitably repressed, and no man, however successful, can be sure of transmitting his good fortune to his successors. Yet the collision of these two systems gave rise to a society much more complicated than either, divided into a vast number of classes differing widely in wealth, power, and prestige. But little reflection is, however, required to show how naturally and necessarily this came to pass. The distrust of Musalman despotism is constantly deposing one class of officials and giving birth to a second to supply its place. Elsewhere the deposed sink at once out of sight. But in India the hereditary principle was so tenaciously held and deeply engrained in the mind of the people that no class could be exterminated by any merely temporary oppression. If nothing else, the tradition of former honours was unfailingly handed on, and with the approbation of the people restoration became a mere question of time. In the words of the famous Fifth Report, ' under whatever degree of adversity ' the zemindars might fall, they had still the consolation of ' preserving their rank and of being considered as zemindars. ' They themselves might come under the displeasure of the

'government and experience its severities: but their families
'would still maintain the consideration due to their station
'in society, with the chance of recovering in more favourable
'times possession of their zemindaries...... Hence it appears
'that even in cases where the zemindar, from rebellion or
'other misconduct was deemed deserving of death, the succes-
'sion of a near relation or of an infant son or of a widow
'placed under tutelage was generally deemed preferable
'to the introduction of a stranger to the possession of a
'zemindary.' The same is true in a less degree of all classes,
and persecuted men have often received from their inferiors
not only 'the consideration due to their station in society,'
but also a part of the rents and dues which they formerly
enjoyed. Such was the tenacity of Hindu custom and sentiment, and herein lay the secret of the failure of Muhammadanism in India. But we must not omit further to observe
that the very extent of the empire involved a much greater
complication of society. Ancient Hinduism was, as we have
said, consonant only with narrow kingdoms. Muhammadanism, lacking strength to do more than partially level the
social and geographical distinctions which it encountered,
could only adapt and multiply them; and that system which
is most hostile to the middle class was the chief means of
creating whatever in Hindu society has the best title to that
name.

The moral effects of this change will come under discussion. Its main legal consequence was the creation and multi-
plication of new tenures in land. As successive proprietors
were imposed upon the land, their predecessors sank into
intermediaries with titles constituting neither ownership nor
tenancy, but compounded of both. Thus we often found a
considerable number of claims upon an estate, and each
claimant took toll from the revenue as it passed through his
hands. But perhaps the most important change in this direction was the approximation to the status of tenancy-at-will.
This had arisen, as we have seen, not only under the zamindars of Bengal, but also under the village 'patels' of the
Central Provinces and elsewhere, and under the village land-

lords of the North-West. This development, always of wide
significance, is but the obverse aspect of the centralisation of
the Musalman empire. In small kingdoms there are few
grades of tenure; but wherever a single government rules
over a wide domain, there, provided that the people is characterised by a certain degree of tenacity and conservatism, this
status is certain to recur: so that we may set down its development in India as not only a result, but an inevitable result
of the long domination of the Musalmans.

Law and its Administration.

We have already seen in what sense we can speak of the
Hindu and Muhammadan law as having exercised mutual influence. The scholastic law of both systems was fully elabo-
rated before they came into collision. In both cases this
differed in various respects from the law actually followed.
Among the Musalmans there had grown up a body of legal
usage founded on precedent, not recognised by the orthodox
books[1], but acted upon by the officers of the state. The
kazi, the representative of the law of the schools, had jurisdiction only in cases of 'civil trials, about marriage, adoption,
'inheritance, and, generally speaking, all questions concerning
'private property.' Criminal cases, such as concerned theft,
robbery, conspiracy, murder, and the like, along with every
offence in the sphere of revenue or other public interests, as
well as all extraordinary complications, would come before the
king's officers and be settled by the law of precedent or the
will of the individual[2]. To the Muhammadan law of precedent corresponds the Hindu law of custom, the latter, it is
true, infinitely more constant and more binding. It was
always recognised by the native books, which charge the
judge to 'inquire into the laws of castes, districts, guilds,

---

[1] Except among the Shiahs.
[2] *Vide* Elphinstone, *History of India* (Ed. VI.), p. 484.

families[1].'   'What may have been practised by the virtuous...
'that he shall establish as law, if not opposed to the usages
'of countries, families, and castes[2].'   The hold which this law
of custom had upon the minds of the people was much
stronger than we can readily imagine, and even at the
present day a Jat, for instance, would, as we are informed[3],
'listen with indignant surprise' if he were told that his
customary law could be made more binding by the sanction
of any government whatever.

The Scho-
lastic
Law.
We have said that the scholastic law of the two religions
exercised practically no mutual influence. As to the Muhammadan law, we may without going so far as to say with Sir
John Malcolm[4] that it was never more than formally introduced recognize at least that its use was restricted. Between
Muhammadans its ordinances in civil affairs would be consistently followed, and the kazi would pronounce his decisions
with just the same effect as elsewhere. 'Public and political
'offences, whether by Hindus or Muhammadans, were tried
'by the same standard[5],' that is to say, in those cases where
any formal rules at all were observed, and all criminal cases
would come under the same category. Revenue matters, as
we have seen, did not fall within its jurisdiction[6]. This is
the entire extent of its employment. Where followed, it
was followed absolutely. Otherwise, it was not modified,
but disregarded and set aside. The law of Islam is the
same at Cairo and at Calcutta. All that was or could be
added in India, consisted of the *fatwās* or decisions of knotty
points by the Ulemas. Of these considerable collections
have been made: but as they are all based on the scholastic
law, it is not possible to speak of them as modifications.

The Hindu book law has been almost equally unin-
fluenced. It is true that 'within the last few centuries,'
perhaps from the ninth century onwards, 'there has grown

[1] Manu vIII. 41.
[2] *Ibid.* vIII. 46.
[3] Boulnois and Rattigan, *Customary Law in the Panjab.*   Introduction.
[4] *Political History of India,* II. 144—5.
[5] Sir H. Elliot, *Hist. of India,* I. 478.
[6] Phillips, *op. cit.* pp. 216—7.

'up a modern system of jurisprudence, or scientific legal
'literature, which compares and weighs, one against another,
'the different views of the authors of the Dharmaśāstras.
'In particular, extensive compilations have been prepared,
'in great measure by the authority and under the auspices
'of various kings and princes, with a view to meet the
'practical want of a sufficient legal code[1].' Of these the
most important are the Dāyabhāga, followed in Bengal, and
the Mitākshara, followed in the North-West and South. It
might be thought that the need for them arose from contact
with the precision of Muhammadanism, and from the demand
of its rulers for a clear account of the law which they permitted the Brahmans to administer. But the discussion of
this perhaps not improbable supposition is matter for specialists
and has not, so far as we are informed, been entered upon.
The continuation of the above quotation is, however, against
the hypothesis. 'These compilations,' it goes on, 'were mostly
'drawn up in the Dekkan, which from the eleventh century
'was the refuge and centre of literary activity generally.
'In Hindustan it had been substantially arrested by the in-
'roads and ravages of the Muhammadans; and it is only
'within the last three centuries that it has again returned
'thither, especially to Kāsī (Benares) and Bengal.' In any
case some beginning had already been made in Hindu times
as we may see from the more scientific character of Nārada,
for instance, as compared with Manu.

Apart from this vague and hypothetical influence, the
Hindu law may be said to have been almost entirely unin-
fluenced by the Muhammadan. Yet we should not omit to
mention that certain slight changes in detail may be due
to this cause. An instance is mentioned by Cowell in his
Tagore Law Lectures for 1870 (p. 215) in connection with the
rules for adoption.

The Hindu customary law, on the other hand, and the *The Cus-*
Muhammadan law of precedent, must have greatly affected *tomary and*
each other, and both must have been influenced by the law of *Precedent*
the schools. This interaction would be most in evidence where *Laws.*

[1] Weber, *History of Indian Literature*, Trans. p. 282.

conversions were common. 'With regard to the Muham-
'madans,' we are told, 'their law, although held by many to
'be a divine rule of life, is followed in many instances by
'inhabitants of this province (the Panjab) amongst whom
'customs in variation of it are inveterate; and many here
'subscribe to laws of property forming part of the village
'system which are not known in the *shera.* For instance,
'they frequently recognize the widow's interest for life in
'village lands and not her absolute interest in a portion of
'what her deceased husband possessed[1].'

But, while there can be no doubt that such mutual
influence was exerted, it is to be feared that the time has
not yet come for carrying the inquiry into details. The
customary law is of infinite variety. There are customs of
tribes, of kingdoms, of villages, of families, of offices, in short,
wherever there has been continuity and succession, there
customary law is to be found. The business of collecting,
comparing, and codifying this law has scarcely commenced.
The very idea of making the attempt is of recent date[2], and
for its fulfilment we are driven to look to the future.

*Adminis-
tration.*
The administration of the Hindu law rested partly in the
hands of the village officers, elected arbiters, and heads of
castes, partly with the servants and representatives of the
king. The former class of cases concerned adoption, inheritance, marriage, boundaries and the like, and were always
liable to be decided as much by the Brahmanical doctrines
as by local customs. Where the two were at variance, the
victory would be decided by local circumstances. The latter
class included all criminal cases and all those in which
revenue interests were concerned. The Kshatriyas and
whatever classes held corresponding rights where the Kshatriyas had never existed or had disappeared administered
their 'feuds' without interference from the king. Under
the Muhammadans the same system in all its main outlines
remained in force. The criminal law of Islam at once superseded that of the natives, wherever the Musalman power

[1] Boulnois and Rattigan, *Customary Law in the Panjab*, p. 62.
[2] I refer to Mr Nelson's proposals.

was consolidated. The old revenue system was retained with modifications, and every officer connected with it exercised jurisdiction in cases concerning their duties. In Bengal the zamindars were required to discover and punish all offenders in their district on pain of themselves making good the injury. All holders of jagirs, commanders of district troops (foujdar &c.), provincial governors, and revenue-farmers were similarly entrusted with summary jurisdiction. In civil cases between Muhammadans, especially such as concerned adoption, inheritance, marriage, and kindred topics the law of Islam was followed, and the imperial or provincial functionary enforced the sentences of the kazi. There remain cases of disputes between Hindus depending on their law or custom. These the Musalmans declined to interfere with, and thus the vast majority of cases were decided as of old by the people for themselves. 'In all suits for debts, contracts, 'adultery, inheritance, the rights of property and the like, 'the Hindus—being left without any form of law or any 'established judicatory to appeal to—had to accommodate 'their own differences, and therefore maintained *panchāyats*, 'or arbitration committees, in full efficiency. It was fortunate 'under these circumstances that the public opinion of the 'caste, as expressed in these domestic and self-constituted '*fora*, operated more strongly upon their minds, sentiments, 'and actions than rewards and punishments from higher and 'holier sanctions[1].'

Briefly summarizing this necessarily fragmentary account, *Summary.* we may point out that while in the West, where the State has vindicated its independence of the Church, law is derived from the enactments of the sovereign power and is administered by its officers, in the East it is deduced from inspired scriptures and administered by theologians ; whence it was scarcely possible for the Hindu and Muhammadan law to exercise direct mutual influence. It is yet possible that the demands of the Musalmans and necessities arising from their government may have affected the methods of the Hindu doctors. The actual though unsanctioned usages

[1] Sir H. Elliot, i. 478.

of the two sects must have sustained changes due to contact. The Muhammadan criminal law replaced that of the Hindus. As concerns administration, that class of cases which in Hindu times was tried by the king, his officers, and by the semi-feudal nobility passed under the jurisdiction of the Musalman emperor[1] and his representatives, whether jagirdars or military and fiscal officers. The Hindus were left to settle their own civil disputes.

Thus the Musalman law was very incompletely applied. Even the *jizya*, the tax on infidels, was never permanently enforced. It was formally abolished by Akbar, and under his successors it was several times reimposed only to be again removed. On the whole subject Ferishta has an interesting dialogue between Ala-ud-din and the kazi Mughis-ud-din. After a long discussion as to how far the emperor's acts were justified by the law of Islam 'the kazy, overpowered by the 'language and manner of the king, got up, and went as far 'as the threshold of the hall, where he prostrated himself, 'and as he rose pronounced, "O king, all that thou doest 'is contrary to the law;"' with which he absconded. The emperor, after his fury had abated, conferred munificent gifts on the kazi, adding these words:—'Although I have 'not had the advantage of reading books like yourself, I 'can never forget that I was born the son of a Mussulman; 'and while I am quite prepared to admit the truth of all 'you say, yet, if the doctrines which you call law were put 'in practice, they alone would not answer the purpose of 'government, and more particularly such a government as 'this of Hindoostan. Unless severe punishments were in-'flicted for crimes they could never be checked; so that 'while I act with rigour in all such cases, according to the 'best of my judgment, I place reliance on God, that, if I 'have erred, the door of mercy will be open to me a repentant 'sinner[2].'

---

[1] Who, like the Hindu rājā, was always accessible to appellants during some portion of the day. Jahangir boasts of this in his memoirs and the fact is confirmed by the accounts of European travellers.

[2] Trans. Briggs; I. 348 sq.

CHAPTER II.

MORALITY.

THE effect of the Muhammadan conquest on the morals of Hinduism is at once more easy and more difficult to trace than its effect on Law and Religion. It is more difficult from the less definable character of the subject; more easy, on the other hand, from the nature of the evidence. For, while an artificial literature may easily represent a Law which was never more than theoretical and a theosophical religion, it cannot well divest itself of the impalpable influence of the prevailing morality. Yet even here we have to beware of that kind of credulity which would regard 'Jonathan Wild' as a picture of English morals during the last century.

Of the law of Dharma as the supreme sanction of *Morality* morality and of the *summum bonum* according to Hindu *of Caste.* ideas we have already treated in the introductory chapter. Caste is however in the main rather what we should call a religious and social than a moral institution. Yet since these ideas are not clearly separated in Hindu thought, it would be impossible to write of the morality of the Hindus without saying something concerning the morality of caste. The charges commonly brought against caste as a moral system are those of selfishness and pride. Life, it is urged, is on this theory a general *sauve qui peut*. The active virtues are discouraged: at the best mutual tolerance is substituted for mutual assistance. Innumerable divisions are recognized among men, and fraternity is as conspicuously

absent as equality. It must be admitted that the advantage
accruing to the individual is the general standpoint of the
system, and that caste divisions are more than trade divisions
and imply a certain degree of mutual contempt. Yet there
are considerations which tend to modify this estimate. In
the first place, the theory of Dharma has encouraged a
feeling of charity and consideration towards both men and
animals. The belief that every soul has passed through
endless stages of existence from the lowest to the highest
has resulted in a reluctance to hurt or contemn any kind
of creature. Harmlessness towards all beings is perhaps
the trait oftenest eulogised in the lives of heroes and saints.
It is found prominently in connection with every religious
movement, and in some, as in Buddhism and Jainism, it
is often carried to ridiculous extremes. Nor can it be
denied that this is a genuine characteristic of the 'mild
Hindu.' No daily meal is eaten without a few handfuls
being strewn on the ground for the birds. Even snakes,
the great pest of India, are in spite of government rewards,
killed only with reluctance. The English traveller who puts
an end to the depredations of the man-eater, the terror of
a whole district, commonly meets with scant gratitude. It
is true that the rayat's cow is accorded more reverence than
consideration. But still it is beyond question in the matter
of humanity towards the lower animals India may even
now supply a lesson to the West. The same spirit appears
in that external courtesy between man and man which is
so characteristic of India. A second concomitant of caste
is general contentment. The life of the poor in India is
as hard as life can anywhere be. Yet happiness and content
are a marked characteristic of that life[1]. This is a spirit
which caste has always fostered. A man's status is fixed
by destiny and by his own acts in former lives, and, since
it can only be altered in a future state, why should he
not make the best of this life? Accordingly it is found that
the low-caste man, so far from feeling discontent and a sense

[1] If any one doubts this let him read the article on the "Mahratta
Plough" in a recent number of the *Asiatic Quarterly Journal.*

of degradation, is actually proud of his occupation and could not be induced to abandon it.

The positive morality connected with the old Hindu system presents a strange mixture of ceremonial and ethical injunctions. Adultery is forbidden along with treading on a Brahman's shadow, theft by the side of omission to rinse the mouth, drunkenness together with allowing one's younger brother to marry first. All these offences are catalogued in the lists of the priests; to each transgression is assigned its proper effect in a future birth; each may be neutralized by the proper payment or penance.

Such was the character of caste as a moral system. Let *Actual changes in the Sphere of Morals.* us now enquire into the actual morality of the people in pre-Muhammadan times, in order to see how both the theory and the reality were affected by the subjugation. It need not be repeated that precision on such a matter is out of the question. India is a continent inhabited by races of widely different stocks and stages of civilisation. Yet such testimony as we possess does afford us a glimpse of a not unpleasing picture.

Europeans who live in India are generally surprised at *1. Honesty and Truthfulness.* more than one item in the Greek descriptions of the society which Alexander and his successors encountered in India. But none of these statements is so surprising as the emphatic testimony which is borne to the honesty, truthfulness, and general good faith of the natives. 'No Indian,' writes Arrian, 'was ever accused of lying.' 'They prize 'truthfulness and virtue alike,' says Strabo; and again, 'their simple-mindedness is proved in the case of the laws 'and covenants, since they are not litigious: there are no 'suits for pledge or deposit, nor do they need witnesses 'and seals, but they confide their goods without mistrust: 'and further, their property at home is generally left un-'guarded.' These accounts of Strabo and Arrian carry authority, inasmuch as they are based on the information of Megasthenes, who spent many years as ambassador at the court of the native king, Candragupta or Sandracottus. Nine centuries later the Chinese pilgrim Hiuen-Thsang

visited India, and in his memoirs[1] he has recorded his views
on the native morality. 'With regard to the ordinary
'people,' he says, 'although they are naturally light-minded,
'yet they are upright and honourable. In money matters
'they are without craft, and in administering justice they
'are considerate. They dread the retribution of another
'state of existence, and make light of the things of the
'present world. They are not deceitful or treacherous in
'their conduct, and are faithful to their oaths and promises.
'In their rules of government there is remarkable rectitude,
'whilst in their behaviour there is much gentleness and
'sweetness. With respect to criminals or rebels, these are
'few in number, and only occasionally troublesome.' If
we seek for more modern testimonies to the same effect,
we have but to turn to Colonel Tod's *Annals of Rajasthan*,
where a highly appreciative account is given of the state
of society and morals in Rajputana, that part of Hindustan
which has been least affected by Muhammadan and other
invaders. We cannot avoid admitting that honesty and
truthfulness were virtues characteristic of Hindu morality[2].
The word 'satya,' 'truthful,' is an epithet which is never
omitted from the descriptions of heroes in Sanskrit books,

---

[1] First translated (into French) by M. Stanislas Julien. I quote from
Mr Beal's translation into English in his *Buddhist Records of the Western
World*, I. 83.

[2] The Arabian geographer Edrisi and the Italian traveller Marco Polo
both testify to the same characteristic of native morals. The former
(quoted by Rehatsek, 'Early Moslem Accounts of Hinduism,' Asiatic Society's
Journal (Bombay Branch), vol. XIII.) writes as follows:—

'The Hindus are naturally inclined to justice, and they never swerve
'from it in their acts. Their good faith, loyalty, their faithfulness to
'engagements, are known; they are so renowned for their good qualities
'that men crowd to them from everywhere, and their country flourishes, and
'their situation prospers.'

Marco Polo writes (c. xxv.) in the following terms:—

'Westward from St Thomas is Lac, whence the Brahmins have their
'original, who are the honestest merchants in the world, and will not lie
'for anything, and faithfully keep anything committed to their custody, or
'as brokers sell or barter merchandize for others.'

Sir John Mandeville's golden-hued account of India is unfortunately
based on hearsay, and mythical besides.

and the early literature abounds in maxims of the type 'fiat 'justitia, ruat caelum.'

Now truthfulness and honesty are just those virtues *Present* which according to our reporters are chiefly lacking in the *Deteriora-* modern Hindus. Mill's account of the people is understood *tion.* to be one long libel. But even those who know and appreciate them best are constrained to admit that, excepting the noblest races of Rajputana and the North-West, they cannot be relied on in money matters, and that their word cannot be implicitly trusted; moreover they are extremely litigious. This is, of course, in a greater degree true of the towns than of the villages, and should be further modified by the fact that the English do not come into contact with the best of the natives[1]. But with these modifications the accusation must be allowed to hold good.

Now it will be observed that truthfulness and honesty *In what* form just that part of morality which we should have ex- *manner* pected to find influenced by the conquest. There are some *Muham-* virtues and vices which could have been affected only by *madanism.* personal intercourse with the invaders, who were too few in number to be present everywhere. An instance would be all that concerns the relations of the sexes. But the power and terror of the Musalmans could penetrate where only their name was known, and not even the remotest corner of Orissa could escape its infection. Enslavement and deceit, weakness and cunning, are inseparable companions, and we cannot but trace the decay of the sense of honour among the Hindus to the loss of their independence. But there were also other concomitant causes, springing it is true from the same origin. The Musalman rule, as we saw, was influential in adding to the ranks, and increasing the complication, of native society. The new classes were for the

---

[1] Col. Sleeman, who had peculiar opportunities of judging, writes as follows (*Rambles*, II. p. 114):—

'I believe that as little falsehood is spoken by the people of India, in 'their village communities, as in any part of the world with equal area and 'population. It is in our own courts of justice where falsehood prevails 'most, and the longer they have been anywhere established, the greater the 'degree of falsehood that prevails in them.'

most part connected with trade and taxation. Their status
was precarious. They formed the link between two systems.
In order to extend their powers upwards and downwards
it was necessary for them to fight with enemies of two
different kinds, and every weapon was needed to secure a
victory. Can we wonder if, under circumstances so favourable, between insecurity and compromise, deceit and dis-
honesty thrived? It is the classes here in question who
have earned for the modern Hindu his ill-omened reputation.
The rayat has retained much of his primitive honesty and
simplicity. In the third place, there was originally an
element of falsity in native society in the position of the
Brahmans. So long as the ancient order survived, this
element was not so prominent, since the Brahmans were
still real moral teachers, and especially in their hermitages did their life offer a charming picture of genuineness
and devotion[1]. But under the Muhammadan rule, while
the regulations of caste became more and more stringent,
the simple rules of morality tended to lose their force, and
the original element of falsity assumed greater dimensions.
It is in this accentuation of caste-divisions and in the con-
firmation, by favour and by persecution, of Brahmanical
privileges, that we may see a third cause of the decay of
honesty and truthfulness among the Hindus.

2. *The
fiercer
passions.*
A second side of morality in which we should expect
to trace the effects of the Muhammadan rule is all that
concerns the fiercer passions. Musalman government everywhere promotes violence and bloodshed. It has often been
the first act of a sultan to murder all the possible rivals
of his own family. Dynasties rise rapidly to be quickly
destroyed. Frequently the ruler is the nominee of the
household troops, whose insolence, after a reign of bloodshed and disorder, is ended only by their extirpation. In
India, which was never completely subjugated, the Musalman rule was attended with even greater disorder than
elsewhere. Every zamindar was a possible or suspected

---

[1] Cf. the beautiful scenes depicted in Kālidāsas, 'Sakuntala,' in the
Rāmāyana, and elsewhere.

rebel. His grandfather or father had often been a successful freebooter who had made terms with the government.
Crimes of violence, the acts of individuals or of gangs, were
everyday events, not to be repressed by the extremest
penalties. In short, under a bad emperor anarchy was
everywhere, and even the strongest and most enlightened
could not entirely uproot it.

This disorder has left a deep impress on Hindu morality.
It is not easy to set in a clear light the effects of anarchy.
But, fortunately, there is one phenomenon of wide significance as touching the change we are considering, I mean
the profession of *thagi* and *pindari*. I believe that there
is in the ancient literature no trace of castes[1] of professional
murderers, whose occupation, descending from father to son,
was regarded as a service acceptable to heaven. Yet the
thags and *pindaris*, who were with difficulty suppressed, the
former under Lord Bentinck in the years 1826—35, the
latter much more recently, were men who committed the
most horrible and cold-blooded murders, accompanied with
every circumstance of premeditation and treachery, under
the conviction that they were doing the pleasure of the
greatest of the Hindu goddesses[2]. This fact might be
thought to supply all the testimony we need. But it is of
far more importance to observe that this hereditary profession
was recognized by the community; the *thags* and *pindaris*
were personally known in their own villages, and so great
was their mutual fidelity, and such the light in which they
were regarded by the people, that it was for a long time
impossible to obtain evidence for their conviction. We have
here a remarkable testimony to the effect which Muhammadan
anarchy had produced not only on the Hindus, but on
Hinduism.

But we cannot stop here. We are driven to recognize *The Kali*
a much wider result, affecting the beliefs as well as the *age.*
practice of the people. Their historical imagination has

---

[1] Though Musalmans were found among the thags and pindaris, yet these
were so closely bound together as really to form castes.

[2] See Sleeman, *Rambles*, I. 304 sqq., II. 6.

always looked back to a golden age of ' truth ' and ' perfection[1],' when the law of Dharma was unviolated by transgression, and the four original castes were happy in the performance of their diverse functions. This perfect society has been, as time has advanced, more and more tainted by sin. The sacred Law and Scripture are less and less studied and obeyed. This is the fourth and worst age of the world, wherein corruption is rife and castes every day grow more confused. The degradation will not cease until it at length culminates in the final destruction, followed by the re-birth, of society. This pessimistic theory has always held a place in Hindu literature. But the Musalman conquest and misrule has rooted it in the minds of the people, and criminals have constantly urged as an excuse for their most detestable acts that we are now living in the gloom of the Kali age, when caste and moral law have been together confounded.

Disappearance of the Kshatriyas: Patriotism.

One important application of this theory must not pass unnoticed here. What the Brahman was to Hindu religion, that the Kshatriya was to society. We have seen that he was conceived of as the protector of the people and upholder of the established order; and that the last function was more than a mere name we may learn from the case of Nepal, where until recent times offences against caste were brought to trial in the law-courts[2]. Now the modern theory holds that the Kshatriya caste no longer exists[3], and though the Rajputs and certain others set up a claim to represent it, the claim is generally disallowed. We have here a clear confession that the theocratic society has passed away giving place to an order based on force. The same is also an unmistakeable effect of Musalman rule. For not only did the conquest entail centuries of bloodshed, not only did the desperate resistance of the Kshatriyas lead to their partial extermination, but, as we have seen, the Musalman government was fundamentally opposed to the existence of an aristocracy of birth and in part extinguished the Kshatriyas,

---

[1] The *Satya* or *Kṛta yug*.

[2] B. H. Hodgson, *Essays*, II. pp. 211—250.

[3] It had ceased to exist even in Akbar's time: *vide* Ayeen Akbery, II. p. 377.

in part converted them into revenue officials. It is true that the Rajputs were long courted by the Mughal emperors, especially by Akbar, and that several emperors were married to Rajputni princesses. But even this encouragement ended with Aurangzib, who alienated a people which had formed the main military bulwark of his fathers' empire. In this way the idea of a paternal government and of a caste devoted to protection and war passed away from the theory of Hinduism, and amid the decay of morality its place was taken by hereditary robbers, incendiaries, and murderers.

With the Kshatriya caste the sentiment of patriotism ceased to exist among the Hindus. It may be questioned whether the feeling ever extended to the main body of the people. But beyond all doubt it was passionately felt by the ruling caste. Honour and patriotism are sentiments which flourish and decay together. In India both were derived from the tribal feeling. Muhammadanism, in stamping out differences of tribe and nationality, involved both in a common ruin. Patriotism has been conspicuously absent in India, and such traces as we can discern of a revival of the feeling gather round the idea of India as a whole and not of any part of it.

In that wide sphere of morality which concerns the 3. *Sexual* relations between the sexes, it is not possible to point to *Morality.* any considerable change either in belief or practice, which we can set down to contact with Muhammadanism. The laws of Manu permit four wives, one from each caste, to the Brahman, three to the Kshatriya from the three lower classes, two to the Vaisya, and one to the Śūdra. But the mass of the people has always been, and is now, monogamous, and only a few Brahmans and rich men indulge in more than one wife. Divorce, even for repeated infidelity, has never been held valid, and nothing that the wife can do can deprive her of her right to maintenance out of her husband's property. Herein Muhammadanism has caused no change whatsoever. The only change we can chronicle in this sphere is that the limit to the possible number of wives has been removed, and cases have been known of old Kulin Brahmans nominally married to forty or fifty girls, whom they have only once seen and who have never been their wives.

The seclu-
sion of
women.

The seclusion of women has been copied from the Muhammadans, but only by the richer classes. Among the poor it is quite unknown. In Hindu times women were not encouraged to court publicity, but there was no stringent restriction. A modern high-caste woman, who should be seen by any but a near relation, would irretrievably suffer in reputation. How far this has affected the estimation in which women are held, it is not possible to say, since the ancient literature is as full of contempt for women as it is of emphatic eulogies. That the influence of women inside the zenana is as great as elsewhere under freer conditions, that they are held in no less tender respect in India than in any other land, is a truth which recent discussions are enforcing in spite of western prejudices. But the ancient dramas imply much greater independence than is now conceded, and in Rajasthan, where, as we have seen, ancient sentiments are best preserved, not only are women better educated and more influential than in other parts, but there are not a few recorded instances of wives and mothers of the true Spartan type.

For the rest, it is not easy to trace in this sphere further direct effects of contact with Muhammadanism. Female infanticide and sati are enormities of native growth, which the Musalman government at times made strenuous efforts to uproot[1]. The debaucheries of the Hindu temples, the opprobrious practices of Ṣāktās of the 'left hand' and of such sects as the Vallabhāchāryas cannot be set down to Islam. Sensuality is indeed the darling sin no less of India than of the East in general, and prostitution had become a hereditary calling in very ancient times. Perhaps we might infer from certain remarks of the astronomer and traveller Albirûni that in this respect also there has been a deterioration. 'The Hindus,' he writes, 'are not very severe 'in punishing harlotry. The fault, however, in this lies *with* '*the kings and not with the people*...The kings make them an

---

[1] *Vide* Ayeen Akbery, i. 302 and Cowell, *Tagore Law Lectures*, 1872, p. 184.

'attraction for their cities, a bait of pleasure for their sub-
'jects, for no other than financial reasons. By the revenues
'which they derive from the business......[1].' This suggests
that the vice was characteristic chiefly of the towns and of
the richer classes. For the rest, though the marriage laws
have always been extremely lax in India, it would seem that
the people have commonly been better than their theories.

We have now traced in three great spheres of morality *Summary.*
the effects of the Musalman domination. Gambling and
drunkenness are vices of less importance, which are vehem-
ently condemned by both systems, and to which neither
of them is in any special degree obnoxious. Indeed in
point of temperance there is no civilisation to which India
might not supply a lesson. Now it will be seen that the
influence here traced can only to a very small extent have
been directly exercised. The moral standard of the two
systems does not in theory differ widely; Islam chiefly
detests sins of frivolity and is lenient to cruelty and violence,
while Hinduism loves mildness and quietism: that is all.
The degradation which we have alleged has been due in the
main to the nature of the Musalman government rather
than to the lives of the Muhammadans, who were too few
in number, and too generally of Hindu stock and habits to
exercise a direct influence on the morality of the rival
religion. Those usages which were least liable to be affected
by the constitution of society and government retained much
the same hold on the people as before. I refer in particular
to self-mutilation, suicide, and other practices based upon
religious motives.

In the eyes of a judge the above might seem to constitute
a heavy indictment against the Musalman empire in India.
From such a point of view it is natural to enquire whether
there has been any measure of compensation. We may
point in the first place to the attempts which were made
from time to time to efface certain enormities such as female
infanticide and sati. But it is impossible not to feel that
much of what was accomplished in this way was of such a

[1] Trans. Sachau II. 157.

nature as to escape the eye of history. How many must
have been the enormities confined to small districts, the
multitudinous offences of polytheism, which the stern rigour
of Islam caused to disappear! We may call to mind a
passage in Albirûni's work which cannot fail to suggest
such a thought. 'However,' he writes, 'I must not re-
'proach the Hindus only with their heathen practices, for
'the heathen Arabs too committed crimes and obscenities.
'They cohabited with menstruating and pregnant women;
'several men agreed to cohabit with the same woman in the
'same period of menstruation; they adopted the children of
'others, of their guests, of the lover of their daughter......
'Islam has abolished all these things among the Arabs, *as it
'has also abolished them in those parts of India the people of
'which have become Muhammadan.* Thanks be to God[1].'
Who can doubt that Muhammadanism has lightened the
task of Christianity in cleaning these stables of Augeas?
But far more generally we may point out how much more
modern a character Muhammadanism presents as compared
with Hinduism. While the latter fades away into innumerable absurd rites and formalities, there is in Islam, wherever
favourably seen, a simple and manly consistency, a fund of
solid and sober good sense which cannot fail to strike any
reader of Musalman histories even in translations. Compared with Islam Hinduism is ancient and shadowy. May
it not be that, as was suggested in the narrow sphere of
law, so generally Muhammadanism has tended to give a
more definite and practical direction to moral, political,
and all other speculation, and that this has been its main
service in preparing India for contact with the modern
world?

Caste.   This brings us to what is perhaps the most difficult of
the questions which we have to encounter, namely, In how
far has caste, regarded as a moral system, undergone a
change? Though perhaps no definite answer can be given,
there are certain considerations which may point the way.
The changes in point of distribution have already been

[1] Trans. Sachau I. 185—6.

touched on. In ancient times caste divisions did certainly constitute a stratification in society, roughly defined and varying in different provinces, but still a stratification in society. To-day only the Brahmans retain a semblance of their original position, as moral teachers, priests, sacred persons. They engage in all trades. Otherwise caste-divisions are now trade-divisions, and except for their hereditary and ceremonial character little more. How then has the change come to pass? We have already seen in part. The destruction of the Kshatriyas, the head of Dharma if the Brahmans were its root, dissolved the ancient society into its component parts, and when this took place it appeared that there was no longer one single Sudra and one single Vaisya caste, but a vast and complicated mass of trade-divisions. This change had begun in very ancient time, but no doubt under the Musalmans it went on apace. The pomegranate shell was broken.

Now in ancient times every offence was an offence against caste. The only distinction was that some offences were punished by the king and his officers, others by the Brah-mans, and others by the heads of castes and villages. All alike, if unrequited, affected the guilty one's condition in a future life. But when the government passed into the hands of the Musalmans, it is evident that crimes punished by their law must have come to be less and less regarded as sins. They were offences against the Musalmans, not against Brahmā, and they passed from the jurisdiction of caste rule to that of imperial law. In this way we can see that the actions of a foreign government must always affect the meaning of caste. Whatever offences that government punishes pass from the dominion of caste. A similar reasoning will show that whatever offences a foreign government declines to allow to be punished, if they cannot be suitably dealt with by expulsion from caste, pass from the jurisdiction of caste to that of heaven. Thus in ancient times, if any man had openly insulted a Brahman, he would have promptly been brought before the courts and chastized. But the Musalmans would not punish such a man nor would his own caste, and the Brahman had to be content with the censure of heaven.

In this way we can see that the range of caste law has been curtailed, and that what remains is but a relic out of a once larger number of rules. On the other hand the strictness with which the surviving observances are enforced is not likely to have become at all lessened under a foreign rule. Each caste being left to defend itself, there would result a strengthening of the class feeling and a tightening of the reins of discipline. Once caste was a great matter, now it was all. Once its regulations chiefly concerned ceremonial, purification, and penance : now they chiefly concerned class and trade interests. As we know it to-day, caste chiefly occupies itself with these. Its ceremonial rules deal chiefly with marriage, eating with, and taking water from the hands of, men of other castes. The religious aspect seems to be becoming less and less important. The trade interest is alive and active.

It is in this direction that we may imagine caste to have changed under the Musalmans. Much passed outside its scope. What remained was of more vital importance and more tenaciously held. The legal and formal powers of the Brahmans passed away with the decay of the Kshatriyas whose business it was to enforce them. Their personal influence and authority gained by the removal of their only rivals. Caste has continued to hold its shield over the institution of marriage, otherwise it has almost ceased to operate as a moral system.

Counter-influence. The reaction of Hindu morality on Muhammadanism is a matter of detail and as such hard to trace. There are very few propositions which can be truly stated regarding the whole body of Indian Musalmans, and it is chiefly in the following of individual and local usage that they deviate from the law of Islam. We should expect that such changes as have taken place would in opposition to the converse changes be due to the direct influence of the conquered race.

Our expectation is not disappointed. The most important peculiarities of Indian Muhammadanism in this sphere concern the institution of marriage. Whereas the law permits to the faithful as many as four wives, and provides facilities for divorce on easy terms, monogamy is in India the prevailing rule and divorce is almost unknown. The latter result is secured in a rather curious manner. It is part of the marriage ceremony on the night before the bridegroom leads his bride to his house for the Maulvi to ask what settlement he is prepared to allot in case of a separation. The young man is at liberty to name any dower he pleases; but it is customary for him to name a larger sum than he will ever be able to pay, and thereby put divorce entirely out of the question.

A second trace of Hindu influence is to be found in the rarity of the re-marriage of widows. A lady[1] who had peculiar opportunities of obtaining information on this point writes as follows :—' A widow never alters her style of dress, ' neither does she wear a single ornament, during her widow- ' hood, which generally lasts with her life. I never heard ' of one single instance, during my twelve years' residence ' among them, of a widow marrying again—they have no ' law to prohibit it; and I have known some ladies, *whose* ' *affianced husbands died before the marriage was concluded*[2], ' who preferred a life of solitude and prayer, although many ' other overtures were made.'

In the third place, some of the atrocities of native morality have occasionally found their way into the usages of the Musalmans. The same lady gives observations on the subject of female infanticide, explaining at once the cause and the prevalence of this usage, which was never permitted by educated Muhammadans[3] whereas it was just the upper classes of Hindus who most commonly practised it. 'In the darker periods of civilisation, the obstacles to ' settling their daughters to advantage induced the villagers

[1] Mrs Meer Hassan Ali, *Observations on the Mussulmauns of India*, 1832, I. p. 46.

[2] Note that this is an *unmistakeable* borrowing from Hinduism.

[3] And which is emphatically condemned in the Quran XVI. 61, XVII. 33.

' and the uneducated to follow the example of the Rajpoots,
' viz. to destroy the greater proportion of females at their
' birth. In the present age, this horrid custom is never
' heard of amongst any classes of the Mussulmann population;
' but by the Rajpoot Hindoos it is still practised, as one
' of their chiefs very lately acknowledged in the presence
' of a friend of mine. I have often heard Meer Hadjee
' Shaah declare, that it was a common occurrence within
' his recollection, among the lower classes of the people in
' the immediate vicinity of Loodesanah, where he lived when
' a boy; and that the same practice existed in the Oude
' territory, amongst the peasantry, even at a much later date.
' One of the Nuwaubs of Oude—I think Asoof ood Dowlah—
' hearing with horror of· the frequent recurrence of this
' atrocity in the remote parts of his province, issued a pro-
' clamation to his subjects, commanding them to desist from
' the barbarous custom; and, as an inducement to the
' wicked parents to preserve their female offspring alive,
' grants of land were to be awarded to every female as a
' marriage-portion, on her arriving at a proper age[1].'

So much may suffice to show that Musalman morality
was not entirely unaffected by the usages of the Hindus.
Yet the modifications which it sustained were and could
not help being inconsiderable. The morality of Islam is
preserved from local influences by the constant circulation
which binds together all Musalman states and by the pilgrimage to Mecca. A pilgrim might not be too well
received if he were known to come from regions where
doubtful or forbidden usages prevailed. No less was it
preserved in India by its own nature. It is definite and
clear, and cases of doubt can commonly be reduced to a
simple question to be settled by the ulemas. In all its
main outlines it is fixed for ever by the authority of the
Qurān.

[1] Mrs Meer Hasan Ali, *op. cit.* i. 349.

CHAPTER III.

RELIGION.

THE theory of Hinduism as a religious system was shown in the introductory chapter to be composed of three great ideas, namely, Reward of Works, Liberation by Knowledge, and Devotion to God. To this theory is attached a vast diversity of cult and superstition. The triumph of Hinduism in India was not accompanied by the expulsion or extinction of more primitive beliefs. The worship of the aborigines, commonly a worship of stocks and stones, trees, animals, and the host of heaven, was rather incorporated in the religion of the Aryan conquerors than suffered to decay. A theory and an explanation was added while the substance remained. Hence it is hard to say what portion of the cults patronized by Hinduism is of external origin. The Aryan of the Ṛg-Veda dedicates his worship chiefly to deified natural powers, sunshine and storm, the blue sky, the winds, and fire. But the later Atharva Veda testifies to a more primitive cult, an underground or popular religion attached to lower and more ancient divinities. These are but seldom mentioned in the literature, but the case of Ancient Greece and other countries warns us against the inference that the lower superstitions were less primitive or less influential than the higher religion of the literature. Yet it is not improbable that the tree and serpent worship, the devil worship, the cult of inanimate objects, are in the mass non-Aryan and aboriginal. The elephant-shaped Ganeṣa, the god of luck, who removes obstacles and grants success to enterprises may boast a similar origin. But a far more potent divinity must be associated with him. Śiva, the peculiar god of the Brahmans, a member of the Hindu Trinity, and often identified with the supreme spirit himself, seems to owe his terrible attributes to the modes of thought of the wild tribes which Brahmanism conquered[1]. The fact that his worship is most prevalent in the south is only one indication among many of this truth. Vishṇu, on the contrary, and his chief incarnations, Rāma and Kṛshṇa, present a much more distinctively Brahmanical appearance; while Śāktism, with its admixture of primitive notions and deep speculation, must be regarded as representing both sides of the native faiths.

Thus the religion which presented itself to the Muhammadan invaders of India was as complete a contrast to their own as could well be imagined, a huge aggregate connected together and interpreted only by a thread of priestly speculation and the universal presence of the Brahmanical caste. How was the Musalman with his intense belief in the unity of God, everywhere and at all times the same, to understand this motley religion of family, village, and local deities? True that even at the first some educated Musalmans, as for instance the astronomer Albirûni, were acquainted with the native conceptions[2] and could understand that to the instructed Hindu God was One under all the manifestations which he worshipped. But as a cult Hinduism was tainted throughout with two deadly sins, an outrageous polytheism and an inveterate and elaborate idolatry. These were the two great evils with which it was the mission of Islam to wage war to the death.

Islam in India. How then, we must ask, did it happen that in India Muhammadanism made so little impression on the beliefs and practices which it was instituted to crush? The answer to this question demands a consideration of the manner in which the religion was there propagated and received.

---

[1] Barth, *Religions of India*, p. 163 n. (trans. Wood), has observations as to the sense in which this is true.

[2] 'The educated among the Hindus abhor anthropomorphism,' Albirûni (tr. Sachau i. 39).

The wars of the early Khalifs were conducted with a religious purpose, namely, the propagation of the Musalman faith, and their victories were accompanied by the conversion of the conquered peoples. Thus the conquest of Persia under the second Khalif, Omar, was quickly followed by the triumph of Islam and the expulsion of the Zoroastrians. But when the real subjugation of India began under Mahmud of Ghazni, the missionary spirit had departed, and conquest was directed not by the zeal of prophets, but by the ambition of kings. Mahmud was not unwilling to acquire a reputation for piety by the destruction of a few idols; but he never even pretended to a desire to propagate the religion which he professed. Nor did the conquerors and emperors who succeeded him in India differ from him in this respect. Themselves Afghans, Turks, Mongols, or Tartars, they had not the zeal of the Arab for a religion which had been imposed on them, and which they scarcely appreciated. The fewness of the numbers of the invaders, the tributary tenure during many generations of most of the native princes, and the devotion of the Hindus to their religion, cooperated to make Muhammadanism in India, what it never was in the same sense elsewhere, a tolerant religion[1]. Occasionally, no doubt, a Muhammadan landlord would circumcise a village, but for the most part the conversions were the result either of interest or of conviction.

The Musalmans in India now number about fifty millions of people, and they are distributed as follows. Southern India was never permanently attached to the empire, and the proportion of believers in these territories is therefore low, there being in Madras but 1,900,000 Muhammadans among 28,500,000 Hindus, and in Bombay, including Sindh[2], three out of twelve millions. North of the Vindhya the relative numbers are very different. Thus in the North-West provinces there are six millions among thirty-eight millions of Hindus, in the Panjab seven millions to ten

Number and distribution of the Indian Musalmans.

[1] *Vide* Garcin de Tassy, *Mémoire*, p. 12.
[2] Which is almost entirely Muhammadan and supplies about 1,300,000 of the three millions here set down.

millions of Hindus, while of the teeming population of Lower
Bengal twenty-two millions, or over one-third, are at least
nominally followers of Mahomet. Now it will be observed
that to a certain extent these figures correspond to what we
should have expected, inasmuch as the proportion of Muhammadans increases as we approach the western frontier. Not
only would actual immigration make the proportion higher
in the Panjab and the North-West than elsewhere, but the
constant overrunning of these regions by foreign armies
tended more and more to break down the strength of
Hinduism and make conversion at once easier and less
dangerous. In Rajputana, on the other hand, there are only
860,000 Muhammadans, constituting not quite one-tenth of
the population. The surprising part of these statistics is
the great strength of Islam in the provinces of Lower Bengal.
It is indeed a test case. In Bengal the religion was certainly
not propagated by wars or other violent means. The conversions must here have been effected by peaceful influences,
and in the opinion of our chief authority[1] on the subject
Muhammadanism was here successful because its inherent
superiority deserved success. Now in Bengal Hindu institutions were of recent date and of very weak foundation; it
is probable that it was not a Brahmanical, but a Buddhist
civilisation whereby it was first raised from a state of bar-
barism. We have therefore a striking instance proving that,
as elsewhere, so in India Muhammadanism was most successful with the less advanced civilisation, while as a system
of greater compactness and more mature development it
produced a comparatively insignificant impression. Even in
Bengal it was chiefly successful with the lower classes, and
there, and to a slightly less extent elsewhere, the Muhammadans belong to the poorest and most ignorant class of the
population.

It has been said that conversion was effected in the
peninsula chiefly by peaceful agencies. The recorded cases
of persecution[2] are to be charged upon the zeal of individuals

---

[1] Sir W. W. Hunter, *Imperial Gazetteer*, ii. 288 and in his *Orissa*.

[2] *e.g.* under 'Sikunder the Iconoclast' and Mahomet in Cashmir: *vide*
Ferishta iv. 462 and 481 (trans. Briggs).

and not upon any continuous state or religious policy. The last attempt of this kind, the design of Tipu in Mysore, was free from any religious motive. It is interesting to mark how futile these temporary persecutions must have been. Thousands of Hindus were transported to the capital city Mysore, where they were compelled to eat beef and undergo circumcision, the two chief marks of conversion. Nevertheless, when the persecution came to an end, they relapsed and sought reëntrance into their castes. Rejected as men who had tasted beef, they still refused to accept the hated yoke of Islam, and formed themselves into a new caste, which exists in Mysore to this day[1].

Since then such success as befell Muhammadanism in India was attained chiefly by peaceful means, we should expect to find that the Indian Musalmans have clung to a portion of their former usage and beliefs: and this is in fact the case. Thus we are told[2] that in Bengal 'the 'proselytes brought their old superstitions into their new 'faith. Their ancient rites and modes of religious thought 'reasserted themselves with an intensity which could not 'be suppressed, until the fierce white light of Semitic mono-'theism almost flickered out amid the fuliginous exhalations 'of Hinduism.' They formed 'simply a recognized caste' and remained to so great an extent Hindu that they 'deemed 'it foolish to neglect the worship of Kṛshṇa and Dūrgā, as well as other Hindu practices. So little had they been impressed with the doctrines of Islam that they formed a sect 'which observed none of the ceremonies of its faith, 'which was ignorant of the simplest formulas of its creed, 'which worshipped at the shrines of a rival religion, and 'tenaciously adhered to practices which were denounced as 'the foulest abominations by its founder.'. Similarly in Rajputana the Khānzādah 'observe no Hindu festivals, and 'will not acknowledge that they pay any respect to Hindu 'shrines. But Brahmans take part in their marriage con-'tracts, and some Hindu marriage ceremonies are observed

Retention and Borrowing of Hindu Usages.

---

[1] *Imperial Gazetteer*, ix. p. 23.
[2] *Ibid.* ii. 289 sq.

'by them¹.' 'The Meos have a mixture of both Muham-
'madan and Hindu customs. They practise circumcision,
'*nika*² marriage, and burial of the dead. Brahmans take
'part in the formalities preceding marriage, but the ceremony
'itself is performed before the kazi. Their village deities³
'are the same as those of the Hindus. Among other Hindu
'customs they observe the Holi, Diwali, and other festivals.
'Their marriages never take place in the same *got*⁴, and
'their daughters cannot inherit.' 'The peculiarity of the
'above Muhammadan bodies is that, while the *ritual* of Islam
'has been more or less successfully imposed on them, they
'have maintained in structure the social institutions of a
'Hindu clan or family, and that the tribes especially have
'continued to regulate their marriages not by the law of
'Islam, but by their own rules of genealogy and consan-
'guinity. Up to very recently their worship was polytheistic,
'and their primitive gods survived under various disguises⁵.'
Similar cases of intermixture of custom are reported from
all the other parts of India, and we must regard it as an
almost universal characteristic of Indian Muhammadanism.
In some cases that theoretical equality among the faithful,
which is one of the fundamenta of Islam, has so far disappeared that not only have they come to be regarded as a
recognized caste, but they have even been split up into a
number of rigid divisions. Thus we read⁶ that the *Momins*,
or silk-weavers, and the *Pinjārīs*, or cotton-cleaners, have
so little intercourse with other Muhammadans as almost to
be separate castes in the Hindu sense. 'The latter are very
'low, generally wear the Hindu *dhotar* instead of the *pai-
'jāmas* which are the proper costume of the Indian Musal-
'man.' The phenomenon is not however confined to these
two trades, but many bodies of Musalman traders 'behave

¹ *Imperial Gazetteer*, xi. 411.

² *i.e.* Muhammadan.

³ It is needless to point out that there are no village deities in Islam.

⁴ *i.e.* Hindu 'gotra,' or family, including all descendants of the same great-grandfather.

⁵ *Imperial Gazetteer*, xi. 411.

⁶ *Indian Antiquary*, iii. 190, 'Notes on Caste in the Dekhan.'

very much like Hindu castes, put men out of caste, &c.'
Indeed caste divisions seem to be inevitable in India, and
no efforts can permanently throw off their bondage. Almost
every new religious movement has commenced with the
assertion of the unity of God and the equality of men. Each
in turn has come to worship its God as one among many,
and each body has crystallized into one or more sects, and
one or more castes, of Hinduism. We shall have to notice
certain instances later.

The above usages and superstitions are not indeed con- *Sufism.*
fined to the ignorant[1], but after all they fail to touch the
central life of Muhammadanism. They form no part of its
belief, and any strong breeze of fanaticism may strip off
this rank luxuriance, and leave the faith intact in its strong
and stern simplicity. Such a revival we have seen during
the present century, and especially during the last forty
years, in the spread of Wahabism, the influence of which
has been felt even in the remotest corners of Lower Bengal[2].
But there are other and more subtle maladies, which with
constant recurrence have eaten far more deeply into the
life of the faith, and often destroyed its fairest blossom.
The growth of Ṣufism, which commenced almost with the
conquest of Persia in the first century of the Hijra, lies
outside the scope of the present essay. The origin of this
mysticism, and its relations on the one hand to Plotinus
and Ammonius, and on the other hand to the Vedānta
philosophy, as well as the derivation of its name, have been
the subject of much discussion. But, whatever be the
true account to be given of these matters, it is beyond
question that the thought and practice of these mystics
have been influenced by Hinduism; and this influence,
though naturally strongest within the confines of India,
has also left unmistakeable marks on the mysticism of
Persia, the mother-country and home of Ṣufism. It is
natural to suppose that the Hindu conceptions followed in

---

[1] Sir Rd. Temple, *Indian Antiquary,* x. 371.
[2] *Vide* Sir W. W. Hunter's *Our Indian Musalmans,* and *Imperial Gazetteer*
and *Statistical Account of Bengal passim* and *infra.*

the footsteps of the early Buddhist missionaries, and having
found a home among the Persians of pre-Muhammadan times
were by them imported into Islam. In any case they must
have been constantly strengthened by additions from their
original fountain-head in India. It is impossible to avoid
mentioning certain points of contact between Ṣufism and
the Vedānta. In the first place, the great Vedānta doctrine
of 'Advaita,' non-duality, is found also in the tenets of the
Ṣufis, who hold that God alone exists and beside him there
is no reality[1]. Secondly, they conceive of the world as the
reflexion of God, who beholds his own beauty in the mirror
of illusion, becoming thus 'manifest in a series of multitudinous appearances.' This is the *Māyā* or 'Illusion' of
the Vedāntists, who make use of this very image of the
mirror, an image which we may also trace in the *Enneads*
of Plotinus[2]. Thirdly, the comparison of God to light, 'ab-
'solute light, absolute brightness[3],' is common to both the
Hindu and the Muhammadan mysticism[4]. Further points
of resemblance, which should indeed rather be described as
borrowings from Hinduism, are the belief in transmigration
and incarnation, and the resulting practice of abstention
from animal food[5]. Even the peculiarly Hindu religious
exercise of restraining the breath was copied by some of
at any rate the Indian Musalmans[6]. Religious tolerance
is so natural a consequence of this philosophy of illusion
that we might hesitate to regard it as in any special sense
due to contact with Hinduism. It has however been more
consistently exhibited in India than elsewhere. Thus a
celebrated Ṣufi of the 17th century, by name Sabjāni, 'ab-
'stained from flesh, venerated the mosques, performed in
'*budgadeh* "house of idols," according to the usage of the

---

[1] Dabistan (tr. Shea and Troyer), III. p. 281.

[2] *Enn.* 1. IV. 36n.

[3] Dabistan III. 281.

[4] Besides appearing in the Aristotelian and other philosophies.

[5] Dabistan III. 277—8, 301—2.

[6] *Ibid.* III. 306. I find the 'science of the breath' cited, as a conclusive
example of borrowing from Hinduism by Kremer, *Culturgeschichtliche
Streifzüge auf dem Gebiete des Islam,* p. 49.

'Hindus, the *pūjā* and the *dundavet* "worship and prostra-
'tion," *i.e.* religious rites, but in the mosques conformed in
'praying after the manner of the Musalmans[1].' The tolerance of Akbar and his successors was dictated by political
as well as religious motives.

It needs not to show that Sufism is the death of all
that is characteristic in the teaching of Mahomet. His
vigorous and living precepts, the example of his life, his
vivid conception of the personality of God become but a
part of an empty and wearying pageant beyond which the
soul must seek for that which alone is real. The historical
character of Islam, its chief strength, is converted into an
offence. Hence this mysticism is excluded even among the
Shiahs from the title to orthodoxy. Yet such an influence
has it exercised that throughout the Muhammadan world
its professors rival the orthodox ulemas in popular influence
and veneration. Among the Shiahs it is no question of
rivalry. In India the latter bear but a small numerical
proportion to the Sunnis. But during the Musalman rule
small sects were continually springing up, which professed
Shiah tenets, and were more and more influenced by Hinduism. It is indeed in connection with this religion that we
find the most obvious traces of Hindu beliefs and usages,
even apart from the special development of Sufism. Thus
in the sphere of belief the nearest approach which we can
instance to a real mixture of religions, resulting in the
founding of new sects, is to be seen in connection with
Shiahism. The Ismailiyah sect, which has always fallen
under the influence of the religions with which it has come
into contact[2], has in India given birth to the peculiar sect
of the Khojās of Kaćh, whose tenets are a mixture of
Vishṇuism and Shiahism, and who hold that Ali is the tenth
Avatār of Vishṇu. 'Their high-priest is his Highness Agâ
'Khân of Bombay, to whom they pay extraordinary rever-
'ence. They do not go to the masjid, but have a separate

---

[1] Dabistan III. 301—2.
[2] E. Rehatsek, 'Metempsychosis and Incarnation among Muham. Sects,'
Journal As. Soc. (Bombay Branch), XIV. pp. 428 sqq.

' place of worship called the khânâ.' They also follow the Hindu rules of inheritance. Again, the Ali-Ilahiyahs, though not of Indian origin, were, according to Colebrooke[1], numerous there in his day. They hold that at every period of the world God becomes incarnate[2] in the bodies of prophets, from Adam to Mahomet and Ali. They believe in metempsychosis, and hence abstain from flesh meat. They base their creed on two rules, the *Hindu Vedas* and the ' law of godliness[3].'

Fasts, Festivals and other rites.   It is in this connection, as belonging to the same sphere of ideas, that we should mention the changes which the fasts and festivals of the Shiahs in India have sustained from contact with the elaborate ceremonial of the Hindus[4]. This is more especially the case with the great Shiah celebration of the Muharram or time of mourning for Haçan and Huçain, who in India are more venerated by all Musalmans[5] than Mahomet and the early Khalifs. Though this celebration has often led to bloody conflicts between the two sects, yet, strange to relate, the Sunnis were wont until recently to take part in it. Nay, this and other celebrations have been found so congenial to the natives that they often themselves honour them[6]. A great French scholar[7] even finds a resemblance between the procedure at the Muharram and that at the chief Hindu festival of the Dūrgāpūjā.

Pirs, or Saints.   This brings us to the last of the wide-spread characteristics of Indian Muhammadanism which can be said to bear traces of the influence of Hinduism. The worship of saints or *pirs* cannot be said to be peculiar to India. But it is claimed that it there holds a much more important place in the observances of the faith. than elsewhere. Each of the two chief sects has a number of great *pirs* whom it specially honours, but who are however by no means neg-

---

[1] *Asiatic Researches*, VII. 337.

[2] Rehatsek, *op. cit.* p. 424.

[3] Dabistan III. 64.

[4] Garcin de Tassy, *Mémoire sur les Particularités de la Religion Musulmane dans l'Inde*, pp. 7—8.

[5] *Ibid.* p. 9.   [6] *Ibid.* p. 9.   [7] *Ibid.* p. 10.

lected by the other[1]. As for the minor saints, who have only a local reputation, their name is legion[2]. Though it cannot be said that they are exactly worshipped, yet their position bears a striking resemblance to that of local and national Hindu gods or deified men, and the honours which are paid to them, the processions and pilgrimages to their tombs, and offerings of rice, clarified butter, and flowers, are of unmistakeably Hindu origin. Sir Richard Burton informs us[3] that in Sindh the *pirs* often bear Hindu names, and are respected by professors of both religions. One of the most important of the Indian saints enjoys this double tribute on grounds which are curiously characteristic. Salar Maçud owes his high place in the Musalman calendar to the belief that he died for the faith after slaying two thousand Hindus: the latter reverence him because they conceive of all great manifestations of power as issuing from God[4].

One further phenomenon is of too great significance to be passed over here. The Musalman emperors and governors were often led to doubt of the superiority of their own creed or to deny its authority. Thus it was a common saying of one of the ablest of them, Ala-ud-din, 'that religion had 'no connection with civil government, but was only the 'business, or rather amusement of private life; and that 'the will of a wise prince was better than the variable 'opinions of bodies of men[5].' But the most conspicuous example was the greatest of all the emperors, Akbar, who even attempted to establish a new religion. An enquirer from his early years, he was wont on becoming emperor to hold weekly gatherings, at which professors of all religions were invited to discuss their views, Sunnis, Shiahs, Sufis, Zoroastrians, Hindus, Jains, Buddhists, and Christians. Their arguments and discussions led Akbar to doubt the

Scepticism in high places.

---

[1] Garcin de Tassy, *Mémoire*, p. 12.
[2] *Ibid.* p. 18.
[3] Sindh, pp. 324—5.
[4] Garcin de Tassy, p. 79.
[5] Ferishta (trans. Briggs), I. 347.

sole authority of Mahomet, 'and a dreadful idea became
'fixed in his mind as firmly as letters engraved on stone,
'namely, that wise men exist in all religions, and that asceti-
'cism, miracles, and prophecies were practised among all
'nations, and that therefore the truth, which is in all places,
'cannot be confined to a religion which is of recent origin,
'and has not yet survived one thousand years, and that
'therefore it is futile to favour one religion more than an-
'other without any proofs of its superiority[1].' It was not
long before he propounded a religion of his own, consisting
of a mixture of Ṣufism, Vedantism, Hinduism, Zoroastrianism, and Muhammadanism. The prophecy that after a
thousand years a greater prophet than Mahomet would
appear to perfect the religion[2] Akbar applied to himself,
and accordingly permitted various forms of worship to be
used to him. His 'divine monotheism,' while consenting
with Zoroastrianism to the worship of the Sun as the symbol
of the divinity, was of mainly Hindu origin. It upheld
transmigration and prohibited the eating of flesh, especially
the flesh of the cow[3]. Akbar even went so far as to adopt
the sectarial forehead marks and wear the Brahmanical
thread, to assert that the Qurān was not the uncreated word
of God, and to deny the existence of genii, angels, and many
other beliefs of Islam[4]. The institution of this new religion, which was widely accepted among the chief courtiers,
was however due not entirely to conviction, but also to
political reasons. The emperor had conceived the vision
of an united India with a people professing one religion
and governed by one set of laws. To the realization of this
great project the intolerance of his Muhammadans was the
chief bar. Hence he was led to propound a religion based
on Hindu philosophical pantheism, and the monotheism of
Islam, a religion which he doubtless thought to be in some
measure true and which he hoped to make acceptable to

[1] Al-Badáoni (trans. Rehatsek), 'Akbar's Repudiation of Esslám,' p. 20.
[2] i.e. the Muhammad Mahdi.
[3] Al-Badáoni, p. 26.
[4] Ibid. p. 34.

both classes of his subjects. If the enterprise was hopeless from the first, and if on the accession of the stricter Jahangir the ' divine monotheism' was at once forgotten, yet the breadth and liberality of the conception were not unworthy of the mighty intellect and noble character of the greatest of the emperors. His successors, who could not equal his ability, imitated for the most part his tolerant spirit, and under the Mughal rule the Hindus had but rare occasion to complain of at any rate unprovoked persecution.

We are now in a position to summarize the changes *Summary.* whereby Muhammadanism was adapted to a Hindu environment. Among the ignorant, and above all in rural districts, it was little more than a name, and the Musalman was distinguished from the Hindu only by the rite of circumcision. He worshipped at Hindu shrines, abstained from eating beef, followed the native laws of inheritance, and was married with ceremonial partly Hindu and partly Muhammadan. Often the rudiments of caste-divisions were discernible. On the practice of the religion in general the effect of contact with Hinduism was to add forms and elaborate ceremonial of every kind, in the midst of which the original meaning of its rites was not rarely obscured. The tenets, if not the name, of the Shiahs obtained wide acceptance. Ali and his sons Haçan and Huçain were held in greater honour than Mahomet and the early Khalifs. The Ṣufi mysticism and its characteristic observances often took a Hindu tinge, and the same can be said of the honour shown to saints and devotees. Rationalism was not uncommon among the educated. In general there was a rubbing down of edges, and the tolerant indifference of the Hindu tended at every stage to soften the harshness of Musulman fanaticism.

If then Islam was in these various ways modified by con- *Reaction upon Hinduism.* tact with Hinduism, let us now enquire in what degree it exercised a counter-influence. In religion, as in other spheres, there is but little trace of effects directly produced by the former system on the latter. Indirectly it was the cause of far-reaching modifications. It has been shown that the vast body of Hinduism has been on the one hand more or less unified, on the other hand greatly complicated by the establishment of a single centre of authority at Agra or Delhi. We must now add that this increase in the number of divisions has not resulted in the relaxation of their stringency. The Musalman rule, we are told, rather tightened than loosened the bonds of caste, and we can without difficulty see that this was inevitable. Prior to the conquest there were two great opposing forces in Hinduism, whose rivalry left room for a larger extent of freedom of life and thought among the people. The overthrow of the nobles left the Brahmans masters of the field. Even persecution strengthened their influence: for religion is the solace of conquered peoples, and the Brahmans are the foundation of Hinduism. When the Musalmans ceased to persecute, they began to encourage and employ an order which they had failed to exterminate. Thus both policies tended to consolidate its power, and therewith to emphasize the divisions of caste.

Pilgrimages. This great effect of Musalman rule, that, while breaking down the ancient stratification of society and creating a more composite distribution with sharper divisions, it has yet impressed a kind of unity on the vast whole of Hinduism, is evidenced by the immense processions of pilgrims which yearly resort to the different sacred places in India. The most sacred of all is Puri in Orissa, the home of Jagannath, and here Hinduism has, we might say, found a Mecca. Pilgrimages are, according to a distinguished scholar[1], the 'vital function' of Hinduism. At Puri every sect has a shrine, and the whole Hindu world is represented. Inside the sacred enclosure caste temporarily disappears, and all Hindus, with few and insignificant exceptions, are admitted to equal privileges. 'Elsewhere Hinduism is breaking up 'and crumbling to pieces; here it gains new vitality and 'recovers a sense of its unity[2].' The pilgrimages of pre-Muhammadan times never attained such dimensions. They

---

[1] Barth, *Religions of India*, Eng. Trans. p. 283.

[2] *Ibid.* p. 284.

were numerous and local, while those of modern times well
deserve to be termed national. Doubtless this is not a
development of a day. It was inevitable from the time when
Buddhism first sought to become an universal religion. The
Brahmans were compelled to look for names to cope with
Buddha's, and they found them in Vishṇu and Ṣiva. But
whether under the name of Buddha or of Vishṇu the day had
dawned for an universal religion for all Hindus. Muhammadanism accelerated the process.

But there were other phenomena, in which the same *Person-*
struggle towards a national faith can be traced, but where *ality of*
the direct influence of Islam is more clearly visible. The *empha-*
earlier history of Brahmanical religion is singularly want- *sized.*
ing in personalities. We hear for the most part only the
names of great teachers, and these are fictitious, being either
appellatives or nicknames. How much of the traditional life
of even Buddha is either mythical or common to other
Brahmanical saints? Even where personal influence was
most clearly discernible, as in Buddhism and the kindred
Jainism, this personality was afterwards sublimated, and the
one teacher faded into an endless succession of saviours and
avatars. In fact, the Hindu mind was both too mythological
and too philosophical to be content with a late discovery of
truth by a single individual, and every new religion was soon
driven to assert its own eternity, defined either as immuta-
bility or as constant renewal.

. The personal and historical character of Muhammadanism
has reacted upon this aspect of Hinduism. From the time
of the conquest a host of new sects has been springing up on
the foundations of the native religions, but inspired by the
same personal zeal and often directed to the same ends as
are kindred movements in Islam. Their founders, chiefly
Vaishṇavas, receive extraordinary honours, and are 'regarded
'as little inferior to Kṛshṇa himself, and may even be iden-
'tified with him[1].' The chief among them were Kābir,
Caitanya, and Nānak.

---

[1] Monier Williams, *Brahmanism and Hinduism*, p. 116.

But if this emphasizing of the personality of the teachers is to be traced to the influence of Muhammadanism[1], in their preaching we find even clearer traces of this influence. In the first place, they all emphasize the notion of one sole God, supreme and omnipresent, and aim at the abolition of all traces of idolatry and polytheism. In the second place, they are unanimous in denouncing the institution of caste, and laying stress on the spiritual equality of men. They also admit the Qurān as well as the Veda as a sacred book, and invite all men alike, both Muhammadans and Hindus, to join the society. Kābir himself ranks as a saint in Islam. The influence of Muhammadanism is here unmistakeable, although the theism of these sects was sometimes nearer pantheism than monotheism. But we must not omit also to notice the same striving after a national religion, which we traced in what precedes. It was not necessarily a truer conception of God that was sought, but rather one capable of being received by the followers of both the great religions, and thereby creating a national unity.

Success and failure of these sects.

But, though the character and aims of these sects bear thus clear traces of the direct and indirect influence of Muhammadanism, we must not fail to profit by the lesson conveyed by their success and failure. The followers of Caitanya and Kābir have almost completely sunk back into the general body of Vaishṇavism. The founders are regarded as incarnations of Vishṇu. Caste is everywhere reappearing or strengthening its bonds, and though there are still bodies of Vaishṇavas in Bengal who theoretically reject it, yet there are few which show no traces of its return[2]. Similarly, the Sikhs, the followers of Nānak, though caste was strenuously denounced by their founder and his immediate successors, are gradually restoring it along with other practices of Hinduism[3]. The other sects connected with Kābir and Nānak, those of the Dādū-pānthīs, the Bāba-

---

[1] I derive this pregnant notion from Barth, p. 212.

[2] *Vide* on the Vaishṇava Sect, Hunter's *Statistical Account of Bengal*, vol. I. pp. 65—8: also II. 52, III. 289, v. 55—7, &c. &c.

[3] Monier Williams' *Brahmanism and Hinduism*, p. 178.

lālis, and the Satnāmīs, are too insignificant to deserve more than passing mention. They all profess the same tenets as do the Kābir-pānthīs, and differ only in the name of the founder whom they choose to deify. We are thus compelled to recognize that, though in certain sects the *guru* cannot be a Brahman, and though many sects have set forth with ambitious hopes of overcoming caste, yet this levelling doctrine is attaining no more permanent success in India than did the law of Buddha, and Brahmanism is still strong in the heart of its offspring, Hinduism.

Is caste then still in any measure a religious system? In *Caste.* so far undoubtedly that the conception of Dharma is still the fundamental thought of Hindu religion. Yet here too it is plain that caste is contracting its sphere of influence. Originally when the Hindu faith knew of only two paths, the path of works and the path of knowledge, it is plain that for the mass of the people, all religion was concerned with the scrupulous observance of caste law, since knowledge was the privilege of the few. The essential importance of the third way of salvation by Devotion to God was that it offered to the imagination of the people something over and above the dry bones of ceremonial usage. Not that it ever in ancient times showed any hostility to caste. Nowhere in Sanskrit literature is the obligation of holding fast to the sacred order more strongly affirmed than in the Bhagavad-Gītā, the book in which the Bhakti-mārga was first and most emphatically advocated. Nay, it may be said that prior to the Muhammadan conquest, no religious movement in India definitely aimed at the extinction of caste divisions: indeed such an attempt was not possible at a time when caste had not yet shrunk to its present dimensions, but consisted of real distinctions of race and strata in society. Even Buddhism, which has been sometimes charged with the attempt, 'never ' in the slightest interfered with caste in the countries where ' it happened to exist; and not only did it not do so—it was ' Buddhism which in all probability imported caste into the ' countries where it did not exist... The truth is Buddhism ' carried with it the denial, not of the *régime* of castes in 'general, but of the caste of the Brahmans[1].' The formal attack of sectaries upon caste was a distinctive mark of Musalman times and due to the influence of the spirit of Islam. It was only rendered possible by the fact that division, which had once been merely an accident of caste, became, as the institution shrank more and more in scope, its very essence. This shrinkage and shrivelling of caste is indeed the real change which has taken place. We pointed out above in what manner this process had been influenced by the Muhammadan rule. Yet, so far as religion is concerned, it is not so much to adventitious circumstances such as this that it must be ascribed, but far rather to a great internal development and advance. The Brahman philosophers had come in early days to see the vanity of the ceremonies and worship of their primitive religion: they had spurned the beggarly elements and sought for themselves a refuge in the dark depths of mysticism. To-day the people whom they deserted have followed along the same path. The centre of religious interest has moved from the law of Dharma to the adoration of Vishṇu and Śiva, and thus by a simple and natural course caste has been ceasing gradually and insensibly to hold the chief place in religious thought. The once latent ideas of faith and morality are separating and taking form, and caste, while not set aside, is a third and narrower thing with other and special interests. So the Phratries in the states of ancient Greece survived into the times of Plato and the Stoa.

It is no objection to this to urge that castes are still formed on the basis of sects, as Sir Alfred Lyall has shown in his *Asiatic Studies*[2]. Nor is any objection to be drawn from the recurrence of caste among the Sikhs and Vaishṇavas. It might seem that we have here a victory over the newer religions. But in reality only so much is true that they have failed in their attack. Each sect that dares to disregard the institution developes of necessity itself into a separate caste, since its adherents, having become in the eyes

---

[1] Barth, trans. p. 125.
[2] pp. 172 sqq.

of the orthodox impure, cannot be admitted to the privileges of marriage and eating together with them. When the attack has failed and the sect solidifies into one or several castes, it is not that its religious impulse has died away. But it is found that the sphere of caste is other than the sphere of religion, and instead of being mutually hostile, they are mutually complementary. This and no more is the meaning of the modern revival which advances so strangely side by side with the growth of the popular religions. Brahmā and the Ishṭa-devatās have made their peace. Doubtless every assault helps to break down the influence of the system. Doubtless the more powerful the sect the weaker become the bonds of the Law. But, though the current of sect feeling is ever increasing in volume, while that of caste dwindles and shallows, there seems yet to be no reason why the one should be utterly swamped and effaced by the other.

These then are the chief ways in which the doctrines of *Summary.* the Qurān have reacted on the religion of the Hindus. Borrowings of ritual, the habit among the lower classes of taking part in Musalman rites, celebrations, and saint-worship[1] are of less importance than the converse changes, since a few additional forms, saints, and gods, while all important in Islam, make little difference to Hinduism. It will be seen that Hinduism has borrowed but little directly from Islam. Wherever an attempt has been made to fuse the two religions, the essence of Muhammadanism has remained apart. Mahomet and the Qurān have contributed nothing of their spirit. The personality of the Prophet has never proved attractive, and the current has always set in favour of Ali, Haçan, and Huçain. Islam might—it is conceivable—have become a sect of Hinduism. For the Hindus the acceptance of Mahomet would have involved an unimaginable narrowing and intensifying of their conceptions. Thus the mission of the Prophet must be admitted to have failed in India. A strictly Semitic and non-philosophical religion could have but little effect upon a system, which was rooted in philosophy

[1] Instances are quoted in the *Encycl. of India*, II. 135, and *Imperial Gazetteer*, x. 372, IX. 289—90, &c.

and rich in speculation of every kind. It offered no solution of the problem of evil and suffering that could replace the doctrine of transmigration. Its God was prevailingly set forth with traits of too solemn and stern a type to attract a soft and sensuous race, which preferred to approach the deity by way of ecstatic devotion. Finally, its paradise was all too gross, carnal, and vividly depicted to stir that sad and placid spirit, really underlying all external extravagances, which hoped only for annihilation of self, rest, and·absorption in God.

CHAPTER IV.

RETROSPECT AND FORECAST.

THE work of the Muhammadan power in India is done. *The Work of Muhammadanism in India.* Strictly limited in its aims and capacities, it everywhere attains the same stage of development, upon which decay and anarchy quickly supervene. It was not from a despotic rule, but from misrule and disorder that the advent of the English rescued the people of India. Sikh, Rajput, and Marhatta were fighting over the fragments of the great empire of Aurangzib. Islam is not rich in men of the type of Akbar, and nothing less than a succession of such could have erected in India one permanent empire under its supremacy. Looking back upon its record now closed we are indeed presented with a striking and thrilling picture. That record, as we view its positive side, is seen to consist in the immense literature which the faith has inspired, in the cities and public works which it has erected, in the glories of the Taj Mahal, in its deeds of fiery valour, in the splendour of its famous emperors, in the great and undying name of Akbar: the whole a vast pageant passing before the eyes of a silent and indifferent people and graven with the motto ' God misleadeth whom he will, and whom he will he guideth.'

But it is in its negative or destructive work that the most important effects of the Musalman rule appear. Its law was never really followed, its morals never attracted the people, its converts were few and but slightly influenced by the doctrines of the faith. But the ancient order of Hindu

7—2

society has been completely destroyed. Political divisions have been in innumerable cases levelled. Caste has been much modified. Religious tendencies have taken a new direction and acquired a greater force and volume. The conception of India as a whole has been made possible. In short, the work of the tyrants in the states of ancient Greece has been done in India on a vaster scale by the Musalman power.

Its Future.   Under the English the Musalmans form, if no longer a dominant, yet a powerful sect, numbering over fifty millions of people. Should our empire come to an end, we might see them again masters of the peninsula. The standard of the Crescent would be raised in the North-West; Pathans and Baluchis would flock across the frontier; and Agra might soon become again the capital of Hindustan. If no greater power should intervene—an unlikely supposition indeed—the history of the thirteenth and fourteenth centuries might be repeated with little variation. The actual future of Islam in India will be very different from this, but what direction it will take is not easy to see. We can only follow such indications as we have. Conversion from Hinduism has long ceased except among the lower orders. The drift towards Hinduism, so far as it ever existed, has been turned back. The after-influence of the Wahabi movement is fast restoring the faith to its earlier purity. The British Government, by recognizing and acting on the Musalman law between Musalmans, and the Hindu law between Hindus, has accentuated the differences between the followers of the two religions. Long before both systems have completely given place to imperial and judge-made law, the opposition will be irretrievably fixed. Thus every cause has co-operated to draw the line of division more and more sharply, and this is the main feature of the problem before us.

Is Fusion possible?   History seems to prove that great and highly organized religions never succeed in extirpating each other. Their attempts meet only with a partial success, and that only when backed by force. Christianity was able to overthrow polytheism in the West; but polytheism was never organized and was scarcely believed in at all when Christianity arose. Judaism still survives. Muhammadanism is to-day uprooting the primitive religions of Northern and Central Africa. Such successes as in earlier days it obtained over Christianity were effected by the sword, and bodies of Christians have never ceased to exist in its midst. On the other hand Christianity has won nothing but Spain back from Islam. Buddhism might have destroyed the polytheistic rites of India, had it been the only enlightened sect of Brahmanism. Against Vishṇu, Ṣiva, and the Vedānta it failed. The Buddhists and Jains still, however, survive in India. Islam, like Christianity in this century, effected conversions among the low-caste Hindus. The system remained intact.

Such considerations may lead us to doubt whether fusion between Hindus and Musalmans was ever antecedently possible. In the Introductory Chapter we endeavoured to show that the two systems were fundamentally opposed. To disbelieve in both is not difficult; to believe in both is impossible. The prospect of union was never fairer than under Akbar, whose eclectic religion was founded on a disbelief in all. His son and successor, Jahangir, was a good Musalman and intolerant of any other religion. The Sikhs, whose doctrine came nearest to a combination of Hinduism and Islam, neither gave nor received quarter in their ceaseless struggle with the Muhammadans, and they are now returning into the bosom of Hinduism. It is perhaps possible that, had India remained isolated from the rest of the world, the dominant sect, overthrown by the Sikh and Marhatta power, might have lost its hold upon its converts, and lapsed into insignificance. But under no imaginable circumstances was fusion possible. As long as the Qurān was read and the pilgrimage to Mecca observed, so long was the severance complete. Mersed in Hindu superstition, the Musalman rayat was still a possible fanatic and martyr. So near and no nearer did the two religions come towards fusion.

Under the English the cleft has never ceased to widen. *Revival in Islam: Wahabism.* Previously the two sects had been content with a passive hatred, and neither hoped entirely to uproot the other. But when under the English communication westward became more rapid and free, the Musalman world began to be more and more sensible of its unity. It happened just at this time that a revival was spreading in Arabia. The great Wahabi or puritan movement first assumed prominence about the year 1784, from which time it steadily increased, until in 1804 its devotees were masters of the whole of Arabia and of the holy cities of Mecca and Medina. When in 1818 the temporal power of the sect was finally over-thrown by Ibrahim Pasha, its spirit was not crushed. Scat-tered bodies of Wahabis are still to be found in Arabia and in the nearer east. But it is in India that it has exercised the greatest influence and has the fairest prospects. At the beginning of the century the reforming doctrines were intro-duced into Lower Bengal by a returned pilgrim, whose followers were named Faraizis. Though themselves of little consequence, they prepared the way for the real author of the movement in India, Syad Ahmad, who, having fallen under the influence of a celebrated reforming lawyer Shah Abdal Aziz at Delhi, was led to adopt views in accordance with the doctrines of the Wahabis. In the year 1818 he caused to be published a book called the Sirát-ul-Mustakim, which 'is in effect the Qurān of the Wahabis in India[1].' The first political effort of his sect, begun in 1820, aimed at carrying on a *jihad*, or religious war, against the Sikhs for their oppression of the Musalmans of the Panjab. The jihad was first preached with great success in Patna, after which Syad Ahmad carried his mission down to Calcutta in the year 1821. Two years later he made the pilgrimage to Mecca, where he communed with the chief Wahabi leaders. On his return he declared himself to be an Imām, and parcelled out the whole of India among his Khalifs. In 1829 he demanded the legal tithes from his followers and began to coin money. But in 1831 he was defeated and slain in battle by the Sikhs at Balakot. His followers, however, deny his death and assert that he is only hidden away to return

---

[1] *Calcutta Review*, 1870, p. 81, whence this account is taken.

again at some future day, an opinion which however is not accepted by the Faraizis[1]. At the present day but few of the Indian Musalmans own the name of Wahabi, but the influence of Syad Ahmad's teaching is both deep and widespread.

In its origin in Arabia the Wahabi movement, which *Object and* with justice claims to be a return to the doctrine and practice *Character of Wahab-* of Mahomet, aimed at uprooting two evils which it found *ism.* prevalent in the Musalman world, the concession of divine attributes to the founder and idolatrous practices. Mahomet was 'a delegate whom we dare not adore, and prophet whom 'we dare not belie[2].' They denied his power to intercede with God. On the other hand, they accepted his life as an absolute guide for conduct far more faithfully than the orthodox, and, while denying the authority of all tradition but the earliest, followed that with unbending strictness. In law they refused to accept the infallibility of the four orthodox Sunni doctors, and disregarded all *ijmā* but such as was collected in the earliest age of Islam. The practices which they most abhorred were the use of tobacco—since intoxicants are forbidden in the Qurān[3]—and pilgrimages and processions to tombs of martyrs, against which shrines their iconoclastic zeal was chiefly directed[4].

It will be understood what a work lay ready for such doctrines among the Muhammadans of India, where Mahomet, Haçan, and Huçain were practically worshipped, and heathen rites everywhere followed. The programme of the Indian Wahabis was framed to deal with both. 'The law of the Prophet,' it reads, 'is founded on two things:—1st. The not-attributing 'to any creature the attribute of God. 2nd. Not-inventing 'forms and practices which were not observed in the days of 'the Prophet and his successors or Khalifs. The former 'consists in disbelieving that angels, spirits, spiritual guides,

[1] *Calcutta Review,* 1870, p. 101.

[2] Burckhardt, *Notes on the Bedouins,* &c. II. 368—9.

[3] Palgrave, *Central and Eastern Arabia,* pp. 282 sqq.; Burckhardt, II. 114—6.

[4] Burckhardt, II. 107 sqq.

'disciples, teachers, students, prophets, or saints remove one's
'difficulties;—in considering them as helpless and ignorant
'as oneself in respect of the power of God; in never making
'any offering to any prophet, saint, holy man, or angel for
'the obtaining of any object, but merely to consider them as
'the friends of God : to believe that they have power to rule
'accidents in life, that they are acquainted with the secret
'knowledge of God is downright infidelity. Non-introduction
'of novelties in religion consists in strongly adhering to all
'the devotions and practices in the affairs of life which were
'observed in the time of the Prophet; in avoiding all such
'innovations as marriage ceremonies, mourning ceremonies,
'the adorning of tombs, the erection of large edifices over
'tombs, the lavish expenditure in the anniversaries of the
'dead, the construction of ta'ziyas and the like[1].'

But how far has this programme been carried out? It is
hard to say. The fanatical Wahabis are commonly hated by
Sunnis and Shiahs alike. The main body of Indian Musalmans
still rejects the imputation of Wahabism, and prefers to retain
its old title as Sunni of the Hanafite school[2]. Yet everything would favour the inference that much has been done.
When the catechism of the Arabian Wahabis was laid before
the Ulemas in Cairo at the beginning of the century, they
declared that, if that was Wahabism, then they were all
Wahabis[3]. Sir W. W. Hunter has vividly described the
rapid effects which the revivalist missionaries have often
produced in Bengal. They have everything on their side,
and wherever the Qurān is accepted there they are in the
right and their opponents in the wrong. The difficulty of
their position is that they are attacking not doctrines primarily, but usages of ancient date in a land where usage is
of greatest tenacity. We may expect not that they will
become a dominant sect, but that their opposition and their
spirit will gradually detach from the practices of the Indian

[1] Taken from the *Calcutta Review*, 1870, *A Sketch of the Wahabis*, &c.
p. 89.
[2] *Ibid.* p. 101. Cf. *Imperial Gazetteer*, IX. 243 (Maldah), &c.
[3] Burckhardt, II. 112—3.

Sunnis the incrustations of centuries[1]. The shibboleth of modern Islam is ' Back to Mahomet.'

Meanwhile the influence of Wahabism is combined with *The Rationalistic Movement.* other forces in a movement of a different character. It is a strange circumstance, but one to be often observed, that for a time puritanism and rationalism go hand in hand. Every religion goes on adding forms to forms, until at last the tide is turned and a reaction sets in. Puritanism, from lack of culture incapable of understanding, rationalism, from lack of sympathy incapable of appreciating, the value of forms, join in the victorious assault. The victory won, they are at liberty to settle their mutual differences, and rationalism succumbs to a new orthodoxy. In India a movement has arisen among the Muhammadans which may justly be termed rationalistic. It owes its origin to Sir Syad Ahmad Khan Bahadur, a firm friend of the English, and until his death the leader of the most enlightened party among the Indian Musalmans. In the earlier days of the East India Company's rule the Muhammadans retained much of their previous superiority of status. The highest offices open to natives were in their hands, and they were held in great esteem by the English. But when Lord William Bentinck sanctioned the introduction of European education into the schools and Persian ceased to be the official language, the command of the situation passed at once from their grasp. They refused to enter schools where their religion was not taught; they could not consent to serve under a government which upheld the principle of religious neutrality. Excluded by ignorance from the service of the state they were left without occupation to brood discontentedly over their downfall and their wrongs. Nor was it the least dangerous aspect of the position that the army was the sole outlet for their energies. They were suspected of nearly universal disaffection and sometimes

---

[1] Cf. Goergens, *Der Islam und die moderne Kultur* (Germ. trans. Berlin, 1879), p. 41, 'Wahabism, consisting in a zelotic puritanism aiming at throw-'ing off the hierarchic oppression and restoring the teaching of Mahomet in 'its original purity, has had a greater influence on Muhammadanism in 'general than is commonly thought.'

roundly accused of sending men and supplies in support of
the Wahabi agitation on the frontier, of meditating a *jihad*
against the English rule.   The Umballa and Patna trials in
1864 and 1871 created a general conviction of their dis-
loyalty, and Sir W. W. Hunter wrote his book on *Our
Indian Musalmans* to bring this danger emphatically before
the public and to elucidate the grievances whereof the
Musalman population complained.   It was on this occasion
that Sir Syad Ahmad Khan first came prominently forward
as the champion of a party of reform which aimed at fostering a friendly spirit towards the government.   He showed
that the disaffection among his people had been vastly
exaggerated, and that the rhetorical assertion that 'the
'obligations of the Indian Musalmans to rebel or not rebel
'hung for some months on the deliberations of three Suni
'priests in the Holy City of Arabia' was a ridiculous travesty
of the fact that the Musalmans had determined to reassure
the fears of the government[1].   Since 1871 he has done more
than any other man to engender the spirit of loyalty of
which he claimed to have proved the existence.   He brought
his co-religionists to see that the remedy of their grievances
lay with themselves.   If they declined to enter schools where
the doctrines of Islam were not taught, it was an easy
solution to establish schools of their own, and combine the
study of Western science with the practice of their own
faith.   The result of these discussions was to create a spirit
of conciliation on both sides.   The government began to
make special provision for Musalmans in its schools.   The
latter commenced an educational movement which in 1881
resulted in the foundation of the college at Aligarh, which
aimed not without success at becoming the Eton of the
Indian Musalmans.   At the present day the Muhammadans
are as well instructed as any portion of the population of
India, and with Oriental Universities at Lahore and Allahabad have but little cause to complain of their educational
standing.   Meanwhile the same movement has given rise to

---

[1] The discussion is quoted in full in the *Life of Syad Ahmad Khan*.   Cf.
Sir Alfred Lyall's *Asiatic Studies*, pp. 240—1.

an advanced party, whose rationalistic tendencies have set it in more or less opposition to the main body of the Hanafis. In literature the party is represented chiefly by the writings of Sir Syad Ahmad Khan himself and of Syad Amir Ali[1]. The note of their teaching is a return to Mahomet, and they demur to the authority of the four orthodox sects. Their connection with the Wahabis is shown not only in the whole spirit of the movement and in their rejection of late traditions, but also in the tenderness with which they deal with the sect. Yet their chief leaning is towards those very Motazalites who imported Greek and other culture along with tolerant and semi-rationalistic views into the earlier Islam. The circumstances of the time, however, have driven them beyond the Motazalites, and in the endeavour to reconcile Islam with modern ideas they not seldom find it necessary to interpret away the literal meaning of the Qurān. Mahomet expressly allows four wives to his followers and sanctions concubinage with slaves: he availed himself of both privileges. But we now learn that this was only a concession to the flesh. He effected all that he could by way of limitation: but his aims extended to the complete extinction of polygamy. So with regard to slavery: he laid down laws and restrictions to mitigate what he could only dream of abolishing. Thus it is clear that there is a party in Muhammadan India which is prepared to go far towards accepting a doctrine of development, whereby alone Islam can be reconciled with the modern world. But can it go far enough? Can it—to narrow down the question—go far enough to give the faith a second chance for India amid the break up of Hinduism? It may be doubted. This very party accepts the oldest traditions with implicit belief. It ranks the Prophet as high as ever and it holds fast by the Qurān. What more or what less can it do? There is nothing in the doctrines of Islam upon which modern education need make any impression. The revelation of the Qurān might be a stumbling-block to the outsider. But no Musalman

[1] Sir Syad Ahmad Khan, *Essays on the Life of Mahomet*. Syad Amir Ali, *Life of Mahomet*, revised with large additions, 1891.

can doubt of it, unless he is prepared to give the lie to the plain and emphatic statements of the Prophet. If he does this, what remains of Muhammadanism? There are no questions of editions or various readings, there is no doubt in any quarter that we have practically all that Mahomet wrote and nothing beyond. There is no dispute as to his claims. Once deny these and Muhammadanism has nothing to teach. Admit them, and we have the evidence of experience to prove that his teaching is not acceptable to any Hindus but the ignorant and low-caste.

The Orthodox. So far we have assumed that the advanced party *could* carry the main body of the Sunnis with them. But of this there is no probability. We have mentioned two noticeable movements, that of the Wahabis and that of the Aligarh school, the former puritan and appealing chiefly to the poorer classes through the agency of oral preaching, the latter semi-rationalistic and addressed to the intelligent by the channels of education and literature. Yet the main body of Musalmans accepts neither propaganda, or so far as it has been affected at all, has been influenced by the spirit of Wahabism rather than by the concurrent movement. This great body may be said to be now in a state of suspense. It acknowledges that the law of Islam is now of necessity in abeyance. It does not join with the new parties in confessing that it is abrogated. It is not actively disloyal to the English government: it deplores, yet accepts not without friendliness, the necessity of the situation. No doubt it is an easy thing to prophesy its sudden overthrow or gradual decay. But there still sits one in St Peter's chair to testify with what measure of ease orthodoxy is overthrown. The destiny of Islam in India is bound up with its destinies throughout the world. Not only India, but Egypt, Turkey, and Arabia have their puritans, their orthodox, their progressives[1]. Everywhere the Musalman world is in a state of expectancy. Outwardly at rest, it is thrilled with every flying rumour, agitated with every whisper that prophesies or announces the end of the present order of things and the coming of a

[1] Cf. Mr W. S. Blunt's *Future of Islam.*

Mahdi. Such is not the state of a religion destined to convert the masses of India.

But how stands it with the other religions which have *Hinduism: its present and future.* now met face to face? It has been observed that in India Christianity and Islam have for the first time met on neutral ground. Never before have they had so fair a field for rivalry as now when both alike are candidates for the lapsed heritage of Brahmanism[1]. Is that heritage for ever lapsed, and shall the Hindus be won, if not for Islam, then for Christ? It is a strange, yet not inexplicable, fact that the great religions have each prophesied their own downfall. We know how few faithful Christ will find at his second coming upon earth. For the Muhammadans also his advent will find Islam at his lowest ebb, and the Prophet is said to have foretold that his followers would be divided into seventy and three sects, whereof all but one were destined to perdition. The Hindus too have their Kali age preceding the Millennium.

The Kali age is manifestly here. The ancient order has passed away for ever, and even its modern and debased representative is, as we have shown, shrinking and waning. European knowledge is at work in its midst rooting up prejudices, destroying beliefs, and remodelling society. Its law has already lost much of what survived throughout the Musalman period. Even those parts which are best preserved, those concerning adoption and inheritance, have been invaded by the enactments of the English. Converts to other faiths and widows who remarry are no longer disentitled to inherit. The son need no longer perform those funeral rites, whereby according to the old theory and etymology he rescued his ancestors from hell. The customary law has suffered in several ways, by the wholesale employment of the Law-books, by the fixity which writing has given to it, and by the inroads of case precedents. The whole is fading more and more into a Brahmanical dream.

The Syad Ahmad Khan of Hinduism came seventy years ago in the person of Raja Ram Mohan Roy. By a significant

[1] *Vide* Sir Alfred Lyall's *Asiatic Studies*, pp. 244 sqq.

coincidence his message to his people was similar to that of
the Musalman reformer and similar to the cry which has
sometimes been raised in Christendom: a return to the early
purity of the religion. Not indeed to Indra, Agni, Ushās,
and the Ṛg-Veda; but to the deep and lofty speculations,
what he would have to be the monotheism, of the Upani-
shads. This would, he claimed, be found not inconsistent
with modern science and thought, or hostile to its study.
Ram Mohan Roy's followers have gone far beyond his position. Most of the modern 'Samajes' have abandoned the
old ceremonial observances of caste. They regulate their
own marriages, and they are active in the cause of female
education. Having practically given up the inspiration of
the Brahmanical scriptures, they are prepared to learn a
lesson from all. Their deism has been described as 'Muham-
'madanism without Muhammad, Christianity without Christ.'
But it is beyond question by Christianity that they have
been chiefly affected. The movement arose from contact
with the English. Its followers have for the most part been
converted from Hinduism by the influence of an English
education; and from Ram Mohan Roy to Keshab Chandar
Sen they have been unanimous in ascribing a supreme value
in religion to the teaching and life of Christ.

*Will it fall
to Chris-
tianity?*   Must not they, then, be more and more drawn to Christianity and in time be gathered into its bosom? Are they
not engaged with far more effect than the missionaries of
all the sects in propagating its teaching? Is not Hinduism
destined, as Dr Duff supposed, to fall *en masse*, and shall not
they be the instruments of its demolition? It is to be
feared that the wish is father to the thought. If any lesson
is conveyed by the discussions in the preceding pages, it is
that every religious movement which has started in India,
has preserved its native colour. Theism never fails to be
tinged with pantheism. Revolt from caste is ever succeeded
by its return. Let us grant that Christ's teaching acquires
daily more and more influence. Let us grant that, as has
been often observed by writers from Albirûni[1] to Professor

_____
[1] Trans. Sachau, II. p. 161.

Sir Monier Monier-Williams[1], that there are resemblances both in moral and in religious doctrine between Christianity and certain forms of Hinduism, especially Vaishnavism. Let us grant that the ideas of a Trinity and of an Incarnation are of great antiquity in India. Yet after all the resemblance is partly nominal and wholly superficial. The mind of the Hindu is differently constructed from the mind of the European, and the two must always be at cross purposes. European Christianity is still an interpretation of the teaching of Jesus by the light of the sober Hellenic spirit. But the pessimism, the pantheism, the feeling of the vanity and illusory nature of the world are no accidental fictions of the Hindu mind: they are the stuff out of which it is constructed. Speak to the Hindu of a Trinity, and his thought recurs to his Brahmā, Vishnu, and Śiva: of an incarnation, and he thinks of the *avatars* of Vishnu: of faith and love towards Christ, and he has visions of Kṛshṇa and his shepherdesses or of other forms of ecstatic devotion. Even should we make large demands on our credulity and admit that the Hindus will be brought in time to accept the religion of Christ, yet the change will be merely one of name. Christ will supersede Vishnu and Kṛshṇa and Rāma: but he will inherit their attributes and functions. To bring Christianity home to the Hindus in the same sense as that in which it appeals to Europeans it would be necessary first to europeanize their whole nature. When Keshab Chandar Sen, the leader of the Brāhma-samāj, declared in the course of an impassioned discourse preached at Calcutta in 1880 that 'none but Jesus, none but Jesus, none but Jesus ever 'deserved this bright, this precious diadem, India, and Jesus 'shall have it,' he went on to pourtray Him as the true Yogi, the ideal towards which the religious thought of India has ever tended[2].

Thus it does not appear that the first or indeed the main object of Christian endeavour is to force upon the Hindus what can at the best be a nominal acceptance of Christian

---

[1] *Vedism*, &c. pp. 58 and 96.
[2] *Ibid.* pp. 514—5.

dogma. It is of more importance that they should accept the
Bible than that they should accept the mere name of Christ.
The name they would convert to their own usage and endow
with their own conceptions. They will declare that Jesus
was an Oriental, whom they are more fitted to appreciate
than we. They will point to the variances of belief and
conception within Christendom, and perhaps end by claiming
that Christ's mission was never fully understood until it
found its true home in India. But the Bible has a lesson
to convey which it is impossible to elude or pervert, and
which is especially needed. The mission of Christianity in
India is primarily a moral and not a religious one. Not
that any credit is to be placed in the old fables which
ascribed to the Hindus every imaginable vice. We know
that there are some virtues, and especially the passive
virtues, which they exhibit in an eminent degree. They are
temperate, simple, courteous, and considerate, they show a
patience under labour and suffering beyond any other people[1]:
in extremities they display a courage, constancy, and endur-
ance almost impossible to match. But Christianity has to
offer a character of a more active and helpful type; a life
which does not renounce or despise the world, but accepts it
with a view to making it better. It has to preach, not as a
piece of false philosophy, but as a great ideal, the brother-
hood of man. It has to raise and ennoble the conception of
woman. If Western Christianity retains enough of moral
elevation and vigour for such an enterprise, it has nowhere a
fairer field for its display than in India; even failure is
attended by no nemesis. The feeling of India as a single
whole is now undoubtedly growing. The new sects are
carrying their propaganda everywhere. The National Congress is endeavouring to evoke a common political sentiment.
In both attempts the influence of English teaching is manifest. It should be the mission of Christianity to set itself
to inspire both with that spirit of mutual helpfulness and
active cooperation, which the teaching of the Bible can
convey, and without which the one will be absorbed in

[1] Cf. Monier-Williams, *Modern India and the Indians*, pp. 154—5, 189—90.

Hinduism, and the other degenerate into a mere agency for wresting power out of the hands of the English.

Meanwhile we are celebrating the obsequies of polytheism *Poly-* before it is dead, and it will not be extinguished in a day. *theism.* It is supported—as a concession to popular needs it is true— by the whole force of Brahmanical orthodoxy. It is in possession of vast resources. It is engrained in the habits of the people. No doubt it will hold out long, and no doubt when it passes away some of its usages will survive under the protection of different conceptions. Not impossibly some attempts to overturn it will meet with a success other than what they deserve. We may yet see the images of Christian or other enthusiasts anointed with daily oblations of *ghi,* honoured with monthly processions of tambourines, and renovated yearly with the costumes which they most affect.

Thus it does not appear that the religious situation in *Summary.* India leaves room for the confident anticipations which are sometimes indulged in. The Musalmans will not be converted to Christianity, or lapse into Hinduism. They will not win over the Hindus to their faith. They will remain an isolated sect, holding sternly aloof from the rest of the population and little influenced by its movements. Probably the faith will make some concessions to modern ideas. It will certainly clear itself from Hindu superstitions. But as long as it accepts the inspiration of the Qurān, it will not cease to bear the stamp which Mahomet impressed upon it, and to regret that its law has ceased to operate. Hinduism offers a different prospect. It is open to those assaults of science against which Islam is invulnerable : it is drawn in less rigid lines and is more supple and adaptable. We should infer that caste will gradually lose strength as a religious institution and that idolatry will gradually pass away. But that Christianity will be widely accepted does not appear. We may expect to hear rather of some great movement in the midst of Hinduism, taking the form of a national religion and aiming at national unity. The slight progress of the Brahma-Samajes may lead us to doubt whether this

rather artificial movement is more than a forerunner of
that which we foresee. But whatever aspect the religion
of India will assume, it will without question be deeply
impregnated with Christian ideas, and will appeal at every
turn to the character and life of Christ; and one of the
greatest achievements of Christianity in the West, that of
bringing morality into connection with religion, may be
repeated under the relaxing climate, and amid the sensuous
influences which mould the peoples of tropical India.

The Political Problem.   Lastly, the religious question depends upon the political,
and conversely. There are practically no differences of na-
tionality in India, but only of race and religion. For the
nations were ground to pieces by the Musalmans, and the
Sikh power, which during this century was rapidly taking
a national shape, has been overthrown by the English.
Hence the eager welcome accorded to the idea of not only
a religious, but also of a political, unity. Is this feeling
strong enough to overcome the myriad race antipathies
opposed to it? The testimony of all experienced men proves
the contrary. The withdrawal of the English would be the
signal for instant disruption. For the Muhammadans would
not tolerate subjection to the Hindus, and the races of the
North and West would not submit to the dictation of
Bengalis and Madrasis. The only real bond of unity at
present subsisting is the English empire, and the only
security for the growth of the sentiment is the continuance
of that empire. Consequently the question resolves itself
into a consideration of the dangers by which the Empire
is threatened. In the first place, then, the Muhammadan
question. It cannot be said that any strong section of the
Muhammadans is actively disloyal to our rule: nay, the
leader of one party has stated that he is prepared to accept
its perpetuity[1]. But it is admitted that their position is a
delicate one. They are liable to be disturbed by storms

---

[1] Sir Syad Ahmad Khan, *Present State of Indian Politics*, p. 39, says: 'It
'is therefore necessary for the peace of India and for the progress of every-
'thing in India that the English Government should remain for many years
'—in fact, for ever!'

arising outside India. Should they find themselves continually losing ground in comparison with the Hindus, they might conceivably conspire with a foreign power to procure our overthrow. Though as a body they have not as yet taken part in the National Congress, yet Musalman 'delegates[1]' have been growing more numerous every year, and it is not impossible that they might unite with the Hindus to beguile us out of our empire in the hope of securing their own ascendancy later. These are indeed hypotheses. Yet it is evidently imperative on the English to keep on good terms with the Musalman population. Nor is this in any way an ungrateful necessity. There is perhaps no part of the people with which Englishmen find themselves more in sympathy than with the Muhammadans, none which equally fosters those qualities of character which the English are best prepared to admire.

Nor are the Hindus, whether the orthodox or the advanced party, unfriendly to the English rule. There is, it is true, an extreme section which conceives that it would enjoy greater power, favour, and sympathy[2] under a Russian supremacy. But that party is insignificant in numbers. In the main the educated are conscious that their very existence depends on the preservation of our empire, while the orthodox are still grateful for their rescue from the Muhammadans. Yet there is no complete absence of danger from either source. From the orthodox: for may they not be led by too great and premature interference with their ancient customs, their sacred laws, especially such as concern marriage and caste, to suspect the intentions of their rulers, to become irritated and discontented? From the advanced party: since it might easily be carried further than it intends either by unconsidered rejection of its demands or by the confidence arising from concessions. From the whole people, because its numbers, growing faster than its resources, tend to make

---

[1] On the 'delegates' *vide* Sir Syad Ahmad Khan, *Present State of Indian Politics*, pp. 57 sqq.

[2] The commonest complaint is of lack of *sympathy* between the rulers and the ruled.

the burden of taxation and the rigidity of the demand ever more onerous and galling.

Lastly, the drift of political sentiment in England has to be taken into consideration. Will the democracy realize its responsibility towards India and its people? Being itself necessarily ignorant will it listen to those who know? Is it not commonly guided by general principles, such as the principle that the nature of men is everywhere the same, and may it not be led thereby to mistake the character of the Asiatic question and set its seal to unwise concessions? Is not the 'unmixed democracy' notoriously incapable of governing, if not itself, yet others, and may it not, if allowed a longer existence than history accords to it, be the ruin of a great attempt? Does not the growth of democratic sentiment sometimes mean that a people is growing really equal in lack of elevation and spirit? Who shall say? Perhaps such apprehensions are purely fanciful; perhaps some of them are grounded in reality. Or shall we really believe that the last age, the iron age of the ancient poet, has come and gone:

> Magnus ab integro saeclorum nascitur ordo.
> Jam redit et Virgo, redeunt Saturnia regna ;
> Jam nova progenies caelo demittitur alto?

But whatever the future may have in store, every Englishman is able to point with pride to the fact that his country in the height of her power definitely set herself to employ her empire in the East not for her own aggrandisement, but in performing what she conceived to be her duty, the elevation of a long prostrate people and the amelioration of its condition. We may quote a testimony which cannot be suspected of patriotic partiality. 'Whoso contests the views
' here set forth, and ascribes the policy of England in Asia
' merely to a desire for material gain, to low and paltry aims
' and conceptions—proves in the first place that he has paid
' no regard to the finances of her East Indian Empire, and
' consequently has not observed that the revenues of that
' gigantic territory never suffice to counterbalance the ex-
' penditure required for fostering the soil, and educating its

'millions of inhabitants. Nay, the truth is commonly ig-
'nored, that England is engaged in accomplishing a dis-
'interested and noble task, namely, in laboriously tutoring
'a prostrate people, whose first act on attaining maturity
'will be to disavow its teacher and assert its own inde-
'pendence: further, that the momentary advantage which
'the possession of India secures to Britain is ridiculously
'petty and trivial when considered as the fruit of a hundred
'years of fighting and endeavour, of such a vast expenditure
'of her treasure and the blood of her children[1].'

[1] Vambéry, *Der Islam im* 19*ten Jahrhundert*, p. 304.

CAMBRIDGE : PRINTED BY C. J. CLAY, M.A. AND SONS, AT THE UNIVERSITY PRESS.

By F. W. THOMAS.

THE HISTORY AND PROSPECTS OF BRITISH
EDUCATION IN INDIA. Being the Le Bas Prize Essay for 1890.
8vo. Price 4*s.* 6*d.*